STOLEN LEGACY

Africa World Press, Inc.
P.O. Box 1892
Trenton, NJ 08607

Copyright © George G. M. James, 1954

First Africa World Press Edition 1992

Cover Design by Carles J. Juzang

0-86543-361-5   Cloth
0-86543-362-3   Paper

STOLEN LEGACY

Greek Philosophy Is Stolen Egyptian Philosophy

GEORGE G.M. JAMES

Africa World Press, Inc.

P.O. Box 1892
Trenton, New Jersey 08607

The author has also written the following pamphlets and articles:

PAMPHLETS

1. Health Week In New Castle.

2. Intermarriage.
   Published in London, England.

3. Black People Under Germany.
   Published in New York.

4. The Need of a New Education for the Subject Peoples of the World. Published in Arkansas, U. S. A.

5. The Probable Causes of Religious Apathy in our Institutions of Higher Learning and the Proposal of a New Naturalism.
   Published in Arkansas, U. S. A.

ARTICLES

1. The Church and the New Mentality.

2. Religion Is An Inductive and Progressive Science.

3. The Anti-Classical Wave.

4. The First Step In Negro Reconstruction.

5. Know Thyself. (A Series of 12 Articles)
   Published in the New York Age and the Zion Quarterly.

6. The Influence of Mathematics Upon the Mentality and Character of Students.

   Published in the Georgia Herald.

TABLE OF CONTENTS

(b) Magic is shown to be the key to the interpretation of ancient religion and philosophy; (c) The authorship of his books is disputed by modern scholars, and ancient historians deny his authorship of the Republic and Timeas; (d) The allegory of the charioteer and winged steeds is traced to its Egyptian origin.

3. ARISTOTLE

(I) (a) His early life and training; (b) His own list of books; (c) Other list of books; (II) Doctrines; (III) Summary of Conclusions.

A The doctrines are traced to their Egyptian origin, as he taught nothing new; B (1) The library of Alexandria was the true source of Aristotle's large numbers of books; (2) The lack of uniformity between the list of books points to doubtful authorship; C The discrepancies and doubts in this life.

CHAPTER VII

THE CURRICULUM OF
THE EGYPTIAN MYSTERY SYSTEM

1. The education of Egyptian Priests according to their Orders; 2. The education of the Egyptian Priests in: (a) The Seven Liberal Arts; (b) Secret systems of languages and mathematical symbolism; (c) Magic. 3. A comparison of the curriculum of the Egyptian Mystery System with the list of books said to be drawn up by Aristotle himself.

CHAPTER VIII

THE MEMPHITE THEOLOGY IS THE BASIS OF ALL
IMPORTANT DOCTRINES OF GREEK PHILOSOPHY

1. (a) The history, description and complete text of the Memphite Theology are given and the subject matter is divided into three parts; (b) The text of the first part is followed by the philosophy which the first part teaches; (c) The text of the second part is followed by the philosophy which the second part teaches; (d) The text of the third part is followed by the philosophy which the third part teaches. 2. The Memphite Theology is shown to be the source of modern scientific knowledge; (a) The identity of the creation of the Ennead with the Nebular Hypothesis and; (b) The identity of the Sun God Atom with the atom of Science. 3. The Memphite Theology opens great possibilities for modern scientific research: (a) The Greek concept of the atom is shown to be erroneous; (b) With the new interpretation of the atom the Memphite Theology provides a vast field of scientific secrets yet to be discovered.

PART II

Chapter IX

SOCIAL REFORMATION THROUGH THE NEW PHILOSOPHY OF AFRICAN REDEMPTION

1. SOCIAL REFORMATION

  1. The knowledge that the African Continent gave civilization the Arts and Sciences, Religion and Philosophy is destined to produce a change in the mentality both of the White and Black people. 2. There are three persons in the drama of Greek philosophy: (a) Alexander the Great; (b) Aristotle's School and; (c) The Ancient Roman Government who are responsible for a false tradition about Africa and the social plight of its peoples; (3) Both the White and Black people are common victims of a false tradition about Africa and this fact makes both races partners in the solution of the problem of racial reformation. (4) The methods suggested for racial reformation: (a) Reeducation of both groups by world wide dissemination of Africa's contribution to civilization; (b) The abandonment of the false worship of Greek intellect; (c) Special attention must be given to the re-education of missionaries and a constant demand made for a change in missionary policy.

2. THE NEW PHILOSOPHY OF AFRICAN REDEMPTION

  1. A statement and explanation of the new philosophy of African Redemption are made; 2. Black people must cultivate methods of counteraction against: (a) The false worship of Greek intellect; (b) Missionary literature and exhibition and; (c) must demand a change in missionary policy.

INTRODUCTION

CHARACTERISTICS OF GREEK PHILOSOPHY

The term Greek philosophy, to begin with is a misnomer, for there is no such philosophy in existence. The ancient Egyptians had developed a very complex religious system, called the Mysteries, which was also the first system of salvation.

As such, it regarded the human body as a prison house of the soul, which could be liberated from its bodily impediments, through the disciplines of the Arts and Sciences, and advanced from the level of a mortal to that of a God. This was the notion of the summum bonum or greatest good, to which all men must aspire, and it also became the basis of all ethical concepts. The Egyptian Mystery System was also a Secret Order, and membership was gained by initiation and a pledge to secrecy. The teaching was graded and delivered orally to the Neophyte; and under these circumstances of secrecy, the Egyptians developed secret systems of writing and teaching, and forbade their Initiates from writing what they had learnt.

After nearly five thousand years of prohibition against the Greeks, they were permitted to enter Egypt for the purpose of their education. First through the Persian invasion and secondly through the invasion of Alexander the Great. From the sixth century B.C. therefore to the death of Aristotle (322 B. C.) the Greeks made the best of their chance to learn all they could about Egyptian culture; most students received instructions directly from the Egyptian Priests, but after the invasion by Alexander the Great, the Royal temples and libraries were plundered and pillaged, and Aristotle's school converted the library at Alexandria into a research centre. There is no wonder then, that the production of the unusually large number of books ascribed to Aristotle has proved a physical impossibility, for any single man within a life time.

[1]

STOLEN LEGACY

The history of Aristotle's life, has done him far more harm than good, since it carefully avoids any statement relating to his visit to Egypt, either on his own account or in company with Alexander the Great, when he invaded Egypt. This silence of history at once throws doubt upon the life and achievements of Aristotle. He is said to have spent twenty years under the tutorship of Plato, who is regarded as a Philosopher, yet he graduated as the greatest of Scientists of Antiquity. Two questions might be asked (a) How could Plato teach Aristotle what he himself did not know? (b) Why should Aristotle spend twenty years under a teacher from whom he could learn nothing? This bit of history sounds incredible. Again, in order to avoid suspicion over the extraordinary number of books ascribed to Aristotle, history tells us that Alexander the Great, gave him a large sum of money to get the books. Here again the history sounds incredible, and three statements must here be made.

(a) In order to purchase books on science, they must have been in circulation so as to enable Aristotle to secure them. (b) If the books were in circulation before Aristotle purchased them, and since he is not supposed to have visited Egypt at all, then the books in question must have been circulated among Greek philosophers. (c) If circulated among Greek philosophers, then we would expect the subject matter of such books to have been known before Aristotle's time, and consequently he could not be credited either with producing them or introducing new ideas of science.

Another point of considerable interest to be accounted for was the attitude of the Athenian government towards this so-called Greek philosophy, which it regarded as foreign in origin and treated it accordingly. Only a brief study of history is necessary to show that Greek philosophers were undesirable citizens, who throughout the period of their investigations were victims of relentless persecution, at the hands of the Athenian government. Anaxagoras was imprisoned and exiled; Socrates was executed; Plato was sold into slavery and Aristotle was indicted and exiled; while the earliest of them all, Pythagoras, was expelled from Croton in Italy. Can we imagine the Greeks making such an about turn, as to claim the very teachings which they had at first persecuted and openly rejected? Certainly, they knew they were usurping what they had never produced, and as we enter step by step into our study the greater do we discover evidence which leads us to the conclusion that Greek philosophers were not the authors of Greek philosophy, but the Egyptian Priests and Hierophants.

Aristotle died in 322 B. C. not many years after he had been aided by Alexander the Great to secure the largest quantity of scientific books from the Royal Libraries and Temples of Egypt. In spite however of such great intellectual treasure, the death of Aristotle marked the death of philosophy among the Greeks, who did not seem to possess the natural ability to advance these sciences. Consequently history informs us that the Greeks were forced to make a study of Ethics, which they also borrowed from the Egyptian "Summum Bonum" or greatest good. The two other Athenian Philosophers must be mentioned here, I mean Socrates and Plato; who also became famous in history as philosophers and great thinkers. Every school boy believes that when he hears or reads the command "know thyself", he is hearing or reading words which were uttered by Socrates. But the truth is that the Egyptian temples carried inscriptions on the outside addressed to Neophytes and among them was the injunction "know thyself". Socrates copied these words from the Egyptian Temples, and was not the author. All mystery temples, inside and outside of Egypt carried such inscriptions, just like the weekly bulletins of our modern Churches.

Similarly, every school boy believes that when he hears or reads the names of the four cardinal virtues, he is hearing or reading names of virtues determined by Plato. Nothing has been more misleading, for the Egyptian Mystery System contained ten virtues, and from this source Plato copied what have been called the four cardinal virtues, justice, wisdom,

[3]

temperance, and courage. It is indeed surprising how, for centuries, the Greeks have been praised by the Western World for intellectual accomplishments which belong without a doubt to the Egyptians or the peoples of North Africa.

Another noticeable characteristic of Greek philosophy is the fact that most of the Greek philosophers used the teachings of Pythagoras as their model; and consequently they have introduced nothing new in the field of philosophy. Included in the Pythagorean system we find the doctrines of (a) opposites (b) Harmony (c) Fire (d) Mind, since it is composed of fire atoms, (e) Immortality, expressed as transmigration of Souls, (f) The Summum Bonum or the purpose of philosophy. And these of course are reflected in the systems of Heraclitus, Parmenides, Democritus, Socrates, Plato and Aristotle.

The next thing that is peculiar about Greek philosophy is its use in literature. The Egyptian Mystery System was the first secret Order of History and the publication of its teachings was strictly prohibited. This explains why Initiates like Socrates did not commit to writing their philosophy, and why the Babylonians and Chaldaeans who were very closely associated with them also refrained from publishing those teachings.

We can at once see how easy it was for an ambitious and even envious nation to claim a body of unwritten knowledge which would make them great in the eyes of the primitive world. The absurdity however, is easily recognized when we remember that the Greek language was used to translate several systems of teachings which the Greeks could not succeed in claiming. Such were the translation of Hebrew Scriptures into Greek, called the Septuagint; and the translation of the Christian Gospels, Acts and the Epistles in Greek, still called the Greek New Testament. It is only the unwritten philosophy of the Egyptians translated into Greek that has met with such an unhappy fate: a legacy stolen by the Greeks.

On account of reasons already given, I have been compelled to handle the subject matter of this book, in the way it has been handled: namely (a) with a frequency of repetition, because it is the method of Greek philosophy, to use a common principle to explain several different doctrines, and (b) the quotation and analysis of doctrines, because it is the object of this book to establish the Egyptian Origin and this cannot be so satisfactorily done if the doctrines are not presented. Greek philosophy is somewhat of a drama, whose chief actors were Alexander the Great, Aristotle and his successors in the peripatetic school, and the Roman Emperor Justinian. Alexander invaded Egypt and captured the Royal Library at Alexandria and plundered it. Aristotle made a library of his own with plundered books, while his school occupied the building and used it as a research centre. Finally, Justinian the Roman Emperor abolished the Temples and schools of philosophy i.e. another name for the Egyptian Mysteries which the Greeks claimed as their product, and on account of which, they have been falsely praised and honoured for centuries by the world, as its greatest philosophers and thinkers. This contribution to civilization was really and truly made by the Egyptians and the African Continent, but not by the Greeks or the European Continent. We sometimes wonder why the people of African descent find themselves in such a social plight as they do, but the answer is plain enough. Had it not been for this drama of Greek philosophy and its actors, the African Continent would have had a different reputation, and would have enjoyed a status of respect among the nations of the world. This unfortunate position of the African Continent and its peoples appears to be the result of misrepresentation upon which the structure of race prejudice has been built, i.e. the historical world opinion that the African Continent is backward, that its people are backward, and that their civilization is also backward.

Finally, the dishonesty in the movement of the publication of a Greek philosophy, becomes very glaring, when we refer to the fact, purposely that by calling the theorem of the Square on the Hypotenuse, the Pythagorean theorem, it has concealed the truth for centuries from the world, who ought to know that the Egyptians taught Pythagoras and the Greeks, what mathematics they knew.

I want to mention here that among the many books which I found helpful in my present work are "The Intellectual Adventure of Man" and "The Egyptian Religion" by Professor Henri Frankfort and "The Mediterranean World in Ancient Times" by Professor Eva Sandford.

George G. M. James

The Aims of the Book

The aim of the book is to establish better race relations in the world, by revealing a fundamental truth concerning the contribution of the African Continent to civilization. It must be borne in mind that the first lesson in the Humanities is to make a people aware of their contribution to civilization; and the second lesson is to teach them about other civilizations. By this dissemination of the truth about the civilization of individual peoples, a better understanding among them, and a proper appraisal of each other should follow. This notion is based upon the notion of the Great Master Mind: Ye shall know the truth, and the truth shall make you free. Consequently, the book is an attempt to show that the true authors of Greek philosophy were not the Greeks; but the people of North Africa, commonly called the Egyptians; and the praise and honour falsely given to the Greeks for centuries belong to the people of North Africa, and therefore to the African Continent. Consequently this theft of the African legacy by the Greeks led to the erroneous world opinion that the African Continent has made no contribution to civilization, and that its people are naturally backward. This is the misrepresentation that has become the basis of race prejudice, which has affected all people of color.

For centuries the world has been misled about the original source of the Arts and Sciences; for centuries Socrates, Plato and Aristotle have been falsely idolized as models of intellectual greatness; and for centuries the African continent has been called the Dark Continent, because Europe coveted the honor of transmitting to the world, the Arts and Sciences.

I am happy to be able to bring this information to the attention of the world, so that on the one hand, all races and creeds

[7]

might know the truth and free themselves from those prej-
udices which have corrupted human relations; and on the
other hand, that the people of African origin might be emanci-
pated from their serfdom of inferiority complex, and enter
upon a new era of freedom, in which they would feel like free
men, with full human rights and privileges.

PART I

CHAPTER I:

Greek Philosophy is Stolen Egyptian Philosophy.

1. The Teachings of the Egyptian Mysteries Reached Other Lands Many Centuries Before It Reached Athens.

ACCORDING to history, Pythagoras after receiving his training in Egypt, returned to his native island, Samos, where he established his order for a short time, after which he migrated to Croton (540 B. C.) in Southern Italy, where his order grew to enormous proportions, until his final expulsion from that country. We are also told that Thales (640 B. C.) who had also received his education in Egypt, and his associates: Anaximander, and Anaximenes, were natives of Ionia in Asia Minor, which was a stronghold of the Egyptian Mystery schools, which they carried on. (Sandford's *The Mediterranean World*, p. 195-205). Similarly, we are told that Xenophanes (576 B. C.), Parmenides, Zeno and Melissus were also natives of Ionia and that they migrated to Elea in Italy and established themselves and spread the teachings of the Mysteries.

In like manner we are informed that Heraclitus (530 B. C.), Empedocles, Anaxagoras and Democritus were also natives of Ionia who were interested in physics. Hence in tracing the course of the so-called Greek philosophy, we find that Ionian students after obtaining their education from the Egyptian priests returned to their native land, while some of them migrated to different parts of Italy, where they established themselves.

Consequently, history makes it clear that the surrounding neighbours of Egypt had all become familiar with the teachings of Egyptian Mysteries many centuries before the Athenians, who in 399 B. C. sentenced Socrates to death (Zeller's *Hist. of Phil.*, p. 112; 127; 170-172) and subsequently caused Plato and Aristotle to flee for their lives from Athens, because philosophy was something foreign and unknown to them. For this same reason, we would expect either the Ionians or the Italians to exert their prior claim to philosophy, since it made contact with them long before it did with the Athenians, who were always its greatest enemies, until Alexander's conquest of Egypt, which provided for Aristotle free access to the Library of Alexandria.

The Ionians and Italians made no attempt to claim the authorship of philosophy, because they were well aware that the Egyptians were the true authors. On the other hand, after the death of Aristotle, his Athenian pupils, without the authority of the state, undertook to compile a history of philosophy, recognized at that time as the Sophia or Wisdom of the Egyptians, which had become current and traditional in the ancient world, which compilation, because it was produced by pupils who had belonged to Aristotle's school, later history has erroneously called Greek philosophy, in spite of the fact that the Greeks were its greatest enemies and persecutors, and had persistently treated it as a foreign innovation. For this reason, the so-called Greek philosophy is stolen Egyptian philosophy, which first spread to Ionia, thence to Italy and thence to Athens. And it must be remembered that at this remote period of Greek history, i. e., Thales to Aristotle 640 B. C. - 322 B. C., the Ionians were not Greek citizens, but at first Egyptian subjects and later Persian subjects.

Zeller's Hist. of Phil.: p. 37; 46; 58; 66-83; 112; 127; 170-172.

William Turner's Hist. of Phil.: p 34; 39; 45; 53.

Roger's Student Hist. of Phil.: p. 15.

B. D. Alexander's Hist. of Phil.: p. 13; 21.

Sandford's The Mediterranean World p. 157; 195-205.

A brief sketch of the ancient Egyptian Empire would also make it clear that Asia Minor or Ionia was the ancient land of the Hittites, who were not known by any other name in ancient days.

According to Diodorus and Manetho, High Priest in Egypt, two columns were found at Nysa Arabia; one of the Goddess Isis and the other of the God Osiris, on the latter of which the God declared that he had led an army into India, to the sources of the Danube, and as far as the ocean. This means of course, that the Egyptian Empire, at a very early date, included not only the islands of the Aegean sea and Ionia, but also extended to the extremities of the East.

We are also informed that Senusert I, during the 12th Dynasty (i.e., about 1900 B. C.) conquered the whole sea coast of India, beyond the Ganges to the Eastern ocean. He is also said to have included the Cyclades and a great part of Europe in his conquests.

Secondly, the "Amarna Letters" found in the government offices of the Egyptian King, Iknaton, testify to the fact, that the Egyptian Empire had extended to western Asia, Syria and Palestine, and that for centuries Egyptian power had been supreme in the ancient world. This was in the 18th Dynasty i.e., about 1500 B. C.

We are also told that during the reign of Tuthmosis III, the dominion of Egypt extended not only along the coast of Palestine: but also from Nubia to Northern Asia.

(Breadsted's Conquest of Civilization p. 84; Diodorus 128; Manetho; Strabo; Dicaearchus; John Kendrick's Ancient Egypt vol. I).

2. The Authorship of the Individual Doctrines Is Extremely Doubtful.

As one attempts to read the history of Greek philosophy, one discovers a complete absence of essential information concerning the early life and training of the so-called Greek philosophers, from Thales to Aristotle. No writer or historian professes to know anything about their early education. All they tell us about them consists of (a) a doubtful date and place of birth and (b) their doctrines; but the world is left to wonder who they were and from what source they got their early education, and would naturally expect that men who rose to the position of a Teacher among relatives, friends and associates, would be well-known, not only by them, but by the whole community.

On the contrary, men who might well be placed among the earliest Teachers in history, who had grown up from childhood to manhood, and had taught pupils, are represented as unknown, being without any domestic, social or early educational traces.

This is unbelievable, and yet it is a fact that the history of Greek philosophy has presented to the world a number of men whose lives it knows little or nothing about; but expects the world to accept them as the true authors of the doctrines which are alleged to be theirs.

In the absence of essential evidence, the world hesitates to recognise them as such, because the truth of this whole matter of Greek philosophy points to a very different direction.

The Book on nature entitled *peri physeos* was the common name under which Greek students interested in nature-study wrote. The earliest copy is said to date back to the sixth century B. C. and it is customary to refer to the remnants of peri physeos as the Fragments. (William Turner's History of Philosophy p. 62). We do not believe that genuine Initiates produced the Book on nature, since this was contrary to the rules of the Egyptian Mysteries, in connexion with which the Philosophical Schools conducted their work. Egypt was the centre of the body of ancient wisdom, and knowledge, religious, philosophical and scientific spread to other lands through student Initiates. Such teachings remained for generations and centuries in the form of tradition, until the conquest of Egypt by Alexander the Great, and the movement of Aristotle and his school to compile Egyptian teaching and claim it as Greek Philosophy. (Ancient Mysteries by C. H. Vail p. 16.)

Consequently, as a source of authority of authorships, peri physeos, is of little value, if any, since history mentions only four names as authors of it, namely, Anaximander, Heraclitus, Parmenides, Anaxagoras; and asks the world to accept their authorship of philosophy, because Theophrastus, Sextus, Proclus and Simplicius, of the school at Alexandria are said to have preserved small remnants of it (the Fragments). If peri physeos is the criterion to the authorship of Greek Philosophy, then it falls short in its purpose by a long way, since only four philosophers are alleged to have written this book, and to have remnants of their work. According to this idea all the other philosophers, who failed to write peri physeos and to have remnants of it, also failed to write Greek philosophy. This is the reductio ad absurdum to which peri physeos leads us.

The schools of philosophy, Chaldean, Greek and Persian, were part of the Ancient Mystery System of Egypt. They were conducted in secrecy according to the demands of the Osiriaca, whose teachings became common to all the schools. In keeping with the demands for secrecy, the writing and publication of teachings were strictly forbidden and consequently, Initiates who had developed satisfactorily in their training, and had been advanced to the rank of Master or Teacher, refrained from publishing the teachings of the Mysteries or philosophy.

Consequently any publication of philosophy could not have come from the pen of the original philosophers themselves, but either from their close friends who knew their views, as in the case of Pythagoras and Socrates, or from interested persons who made a record of those philosophical teachings that had become popular opinion and tradition. There is no wonder then, that in the absence of original authorship, history has had to resort to the strategy of accepting Aristotle's opinion as the sole authority in determining the authorship of Greek Philosophy (Introduction to Alfred Weber's History of Philosophy). It is for these reasons that great doubt surrounds the so-

[13]

called Greek authorship of philosophy. (William Turner's
History of Philosophy p. 35; 39; 47; 53; 62; 79; 210-211; 627.
Ancient Mysteries by C. H. Vail p. 16. Theophrastus: Frag-
ment 2 apud Diels. Introduction to Alfred Weber's History of
Philosophy.)

3. The Chronology of Greek Philosophers Is Mere Spec-ulation.

History knows nothing about the early life and training of
the Greek philosophers and this is true not only of the pre-
Socratic philosophers: but also of Socrates, Plato and Aristotle,
who appear in history about the age of eighteen and begin to
teach at forty.

As a body of men they were undesirable to the state, (per-
sonae non gratae) and were consequently persecuted and
driven into hiding and secrecy. Under such circumstances they
kept no records of their activities and this was done in order
to conceal their identity. After the conquest of Egypt by Alexander the Great, and the seizure and looting of the Royal
Library at Alexandria, Aristotle's plan to usurp Egyptian philosophy, was subsequently carried out by members of his
school: Theophrastus, Andronicus of Rhodes and Eudemus,
who soon found themselves confronted with the problem of a
chronology for a history of philosophy. (Introduction of Zeller's Hist. of Phil. p. 13).

Throughout this effort there has been much speculation concerning the date of birth of philosophers, whom the public
knew very little about. As early as the third century B. C.
(274-194 B. C.) Eratosthenes, a Stoic drew up a chronology of
Greek philosophers and in the second century B. C. (140)
Apollodorus also drew up another. The effort continued, and
in the first century B. C. (60-70 B. C.) Andronicus, the
eleventh Head of the Peripatetic school, also drew up another.

This difficulty continued throughout the early centuries,
and has come down to the present time for it appears that all
modern writers on Greek Philosophy are unable to agree on

the dates that should be assigned to the nativity of the philosophers. The only exception appears to occur with reference to the three Athenian philosophers, i.e., Socrates, Plato and Aristotle, the date of whose nativity is believed to be certain, and concerning which there is general agreement among historians.

However, when we come to deal with the pre-Socratic philosophers, we are confronted with confusion and uncertainty, and a few examples would serve to illustrate the untrustworthy nature of the chronology of Greek Philosophers.

(1) Diogenes Laertius places the birth of Thales at 640 B. C., while William Turner's History of Philosophy places it as 620 B. C.; that of Frank Thilly at 624 B. C.; that of A. K. Rogers at early in the sixth century B. C.; and that of W. G. Tennemann at 600 B. C.

(2) Diogenes Laertius places the birth of Anaximenes at 546 B. C.; while W. Windelbrand places it at the sixth century B. C.; that of Frank Thilly at 588 B. C.; that of B. D. Alexander at 560 B. C.; while that of A. K. Rogers at the sixth century B. C.

(3) Parmenides is credited by Diogenes as being born at 500 B. C.; while Fuller, Thilly and Rogers omit a date of birth, because they say it is unknown.

(4) Zeller places the birth of Xenophanes at 576 B. C.; while Diogenes gives 570 B C.; and the majority of the other historians declare that the date of birth is unknown.

(5) With reference to Xeno, Diogenes who does not know the date of his birth, says that he flourished between B. C. 464-460; while William Turner places it at 490 B. C.; like Frank Thilly and B. D. Alexander; while Fuller, A. K. Rogers and W. G. Tennemann declare it is unknown.

(6) With references to Heraclitus, Zeller makes the following suppositions: if he died in 475 B. C. and if he was sixty years old when he died, then he must have been born in 535 B. C.; similarly Diogenes supposes that he flourished between B. C. 504-500; and while William Turner places his birth at 530 B. C.; Windelbrand places it at 536 B. C.; and

[15]

Fuller and Tennemann declare that he flourished in 500 B. C.

(7) With reference to Pythagoras, Zeller who does not know the date of his birth supposes that it occurred between the years 580-570 B. C.; and while Diogenes also supposes that it occurred between the years 582-500 B. C.; William Turner, Fuller, Rogers, and Tennemann declare that it is unknown.

(8) With reference to Empedocles, while Diogenes places his birth at 484 B. C.; Turner, Windelbrand, Fuller, B. D. Alexander and Tennemann place it at 490 B. C.; while A. K. Rogers and others declare it is unknown.

(9) With reference to Anaxagoras, while Zeller and Diogenes place his birth at 500 B. C.; William Turner, A. G. Fuller, and Frank Thilly agree with them, while Alexander places it at 450 B. C. and A. K. Rogers and others declare it is unknown.

(10) With reference to Leucippus, all historians seem to be of the opinion that he has never existed.

(11) Socrates (469-399 B. C.), Plato (427-347 B. C.), and Aristotle (384-322 B. C.) are the only three philosophers the dates of whose nativity and death do not seem to have led to speculation among historians; but the reason for this uniformity is probably due to the fact that they were Athenians and had been indicted by the Athenian Government who would naturally have investigated them and kept a record of their cases. (A. K. Roger's Hist. of Phil. p. 104).

N. B.

It must be noted from the preceding comparative study of the chronology of Greek philosophers that (a) the variation in dates points to speculation (b) the pre-Socratic philosophers were unknown because they were foreigners to the Athenian Government and probably never existed (c) it follows that both the pre-Socratic philosophers together with Socrates, Plato and Aristotle were persecuted by the Athenian Government tor introducing foreign doctrines into Athens. (d) In consequence of these facts, any subsequent claim by the

Greeks to the ownership or authorship of the same doctrines which they had rejected and persecuted, must be regarded as a usurpation.

4. The Compilation of the History of Greek Philosophy Was the Plan of Aristotle Executed by His School.

When Aristotle decided to compile a history of Greek Philosophy he must have made known his wishes to his pupils Theophrastus and Eudemus: for no sooner did he produce his metaphysics, than Theophrastus followed him by publishing eighteen books on the doctrines of the physicists. Similarly, after Theophrastus had published his doctrines of the physicists, Eudemus produced separate histories of Arithmetic, Geometry, Astronomy and also theology. This was an amazing start, because of the large number of scientific books, and the wide range of subjects treated. This situation has rightly aroused the suspicion of the world, as it questions the source of these scientific works.

Since Theophrastus and Eudemus were students under Aristotle at the same time, and since the conquest of Egypt by Alexander the Great, made the Egyptian Library at Alexandria available to the Greeks for research, then it must be expected that the three men, Aristotle who was a close friend of Alexander, Theophrastus and Eudemus not only did research at the Alexandrine Library at the same time, but must also have helped themselves to books, which enabled them to follow each other so closely in the production of scientific works (William Turner's Hist. of Phil. p. 158-159), which were either a portion of the war booty taken from the Library or compilations from them. (Note that Aristotle's works reveal the signs of note taking and that Theophrastus and Eudemus were pupils attending Aristotle's school at the same time). William Turner's Hist. of Phil. p. 127.

Just here it might be as well to mention the names of Aristotle's pupils who took an active part in promoting the movement towards the compilation of a history of Greek philosophy:

(a) Theophrastus of Lesbos 371-286 B. C., who succeeded Aristotle as head of the peripatetic school. As elsewhere mentioned, he is said to have produced eighteen books on the doctrines of physicists. Who were these physicists? Greek or Egyptians? Just think of it.

(b) Eudemus of Rhodes a contemporary of Theophrastus with whom he also attended Aristotle's school. He is said to have produced histories of Arithmetic, geometry, astronomy and theology, as elsewhere mentioned. What was the source of the data of the histories of these sciences, which must have taken any nation thousands of years to develop? Greece or Egypt? Just think of it.

(c) Andronicus of Rhodes, an Eclectic of Aristotle's school and editor of his works (B. C. 70).

These men's works together with Aristotle's metaphysics, which contained a critical summary of the doctrines of all preceding philosophers, seem to form the nucleus of a compilation of what has been called, the history of Greek philosophy (Zeller's Hist. of Greek Phil.: Introduction p. 7-14).

The next movement was the organization of an association called "The learned study of Aristotle's Writings", whose members were Theophrastus and Andronicus, who were both closely connected with the school of Aristotle. The function of this association was to identify the literature and doctrines of philosophy with their so-called respective authors, and in order to accomplish this the alumni of Aristotle's school and its friends were encouraged to enter upon a research for Aristotle's works and to write commentaries on them.

In addition to this, the Learned Association also encouraged research for the recovery of what has been named Fragments or remnants of a book, which is supposed to have once existed, and to have borne the common title *"Peri Physeos"*, i.e., concerning nature.

Here again those who went out in search of "peri physeos"

or its remnants were the alumni of Aristotle's school and its friends: but their efforts to establish authorship was a failure.

(a) Theophrastus found only two lines of peri physeos, supposed to have been written by Anaximander.

(b) Sextus and Proclus of the fifth century A. D., and Simplicius of the sixth century A. D. are said to have found a copy of "peri physeos" supposed to have been produced by Parmenides.

(c) In addition, the name of Simplicius is also associated with a copy of "peri physeos", which is supposed to have been produced by Anaxagoras.

So much for "peri physeos and the Fragments," and so much for the attempt of "The Learned Association" for the study of Aristotle's works; which has failed because of lack of evidence, as has elsewhere been pointed out.

The recovery of two copies and two lines of "peri physeos" is not proof that all Greek Philosophers wrote "peri physeos", or even that the names assigned to them were their bona fide authors. It certainly would appear that the object of the Learned Association was to beat Aristotle's own drum and dance. It was Aristotle's idea to compile a history of philosophy, and it was Aristotle's school and its alumni that carried out the idea, we are told.

CHAPTER II:

So-called Greek Philosophy Was Alien To The Greeks And Their Conditions Of Life.

The Period of Greek Philosophy (640-322 B. C.) Was A Period of Internal and External Wars, and Was Therefore Unsuitable For Producing Philosophers.

HISTORY supports the fact that from the time of Thales. to the time of Aristotle, the Greeks were victims of internal disunion, on the one hand, while on the other, they lived in constant fear of invasion from the Persians who were a common enemy to the city states.

Consequently when they were not fighting with one another they found themselves busy fighting the Persians, who soon dominated them and became their masters. From the 6th century B. C. the territory from the coast of Asia Minor to the Indus Valley became united under the single power of Persia, whose central territory Iran has survived as a national unit to the present day. Persian expansion was like a nightmare to the Greeks who dreaded the Persians on account of their invulnerable navy, and organized themselves into Leagues and Confederacies in order to resist their enemy. (C. 12 P. 195; Sandford's Mediterranean World). There are three sources which throw light on the chaotic and troublesome conditions of this period in Greek history. (A) The Persian Conquests (B) The Leagues and (C) Peloponnesian wars.

A. *The Persian Conquests*

After the Persians had conquered the Ionians (possibly ancient Hittites), and made them their subjects, Polycrates (539-524 B. C.) seized the Island of Samos and made it a famous city. (Sandford's Mediterranean World c. 9). Between

[21]

499 and 494 B. C. the Ionians revolted against the Persians, who defeated them at Lade, while Cyprus and Miletus were also captured. (Sandford's Mediterranean World c. 12). In the summer of 490 B. C. Greek and Persian forces met at Marathon, but after a hand to hand fight, both belligerents withdrew, only to prepare stronger forces in order to renew the conflict. Accordingly, after ten years had elapsed a Hellenic League was organized against the Persians, and the Spartan King Leonides was sent with an army to hold the pass at Thermopylae, until the fleet should win a decisive victory. (C. 12, P. 202; Sandford's Mediterranean World). Accordingly, during the month of August 481 B. C. Persian ships under the command of Xerxes anchored in the gulf of Pagasae, while the Greeks anchored off Cape Artemisium. Both sides awaited a favorable opportunity to attack. The Persians began to force the pass while simultaneously one of their detachments was secretly aided by a Greek traitor, along a steep mountain pass to the rear of the Greek position. Having been taken by surprise, the Greek guards immediately withdrew without resistance. The Spartans who were guarding Thermopylae were all slain and the pass captured by the Persians. (Sandford's Mediterranean World C. 12 P. 202). Having been defeated at Thermopylae, the Greeks withdrew to Salamis, where again they encountered a naval engagement with the Persians. It was late in September 481 B. C., and the result was a wanton destruction of ships on both sides, without any decision. Both belligerents withdrew: The Persians to Thessaly, and the Greeks to Attica. (Sandford's Mediterranean World C. 12 P. 203).

With the persistent aim of freedom from Persian domination, Athens, together with the island and coast cities (of the Aegean and Ionia) renewed their resistance of Persian rule. This was the confederacy of Delos, which undertook several naval engagements, but with little or no success. In 467 B. C. the battle of Eurymedon River was fought and lost with a great number of ships. Eighteen years later (449 B. C.)

another naval engagement took place off the island of Cyprus, but again without decision, and consequently Persian sovereignty over the Greeks remained. (Sandford's Mediterranean World C. 12 P. 205). In the meantime Sparta, under the terms of the Treaty of Miletus (413 B. C.) obtained subsidies from Persia, for naval construction, on condition that she recognize Persian sovereignty over the Ionians and their allies. This was done by Sparta as a threat to Athenian ambitions.

However, it was not long after the Treaty of Miletus, that the Greeks themselves submitted to the authority and dominance of the Persians. During the winter 387-386 B. C., the individual Ionian cities, signed the peace terms of the Persian King, and finally accepted Persian rule. This Treaty was negotiated by a Spartan envoy who was authorized by the Persian King to enforce its provisions. (Sandford's Mediterranean World C. 13 and 15, P. 225 and 255).

B. *The Leagues*

Apart from the resistance of a common foe, the Persians, a study of the function of the Leagues, reveals the enmity and spirit of aggression which were characteristic of the relationship which existed between the Greek city states themselves.

Accordingly in 505 B. C., the Peloponnesian states signed treaties among themselves, pledging warfare against Sparta who had absorbed them under her influence. Meanwhile, Aristogoras revived the Ionian League (499-494 B. C.) to resist Persian aggression, and friendship between Athens and Aegina was restored by the Hellenic League (481 B. C.) which was afterward converted into the Confederacy of Delos (478 B. C.) as mentioned elsewhere. In like manner, Thebes also fell in line with the general temper of the age and organized the Boeotian League, a federation of city states, for self-protection and aggression. (Sandford's Mediterranean World C. 9, P. 150; C. 12, P. 201).

In 377 B. C. a second Athenian Confederacy was organized, but this was to frustrate the aims of the Lacedaemonians and

to compel them to respect the right of the Athenians and their
allies (Sandford's Mediterranean World C. 15, P. 260). Likewise in 290 B C., the Aetolian League, made up of the States
of central Greece, gained control of Delphi, and frequently
violated Achaean rights in the Peloponnesus, while in 225
B. C. Antigonus Doson organized another Hellenic League,
with the purpose of obstructing the ambitions of Sparta and
her Aetolian allies. (Sandford's Mediterranean World C. 18,
P. 317 and 319).

(W. H. Couch's Hist. of Greece, p. 206-209, c. 11. Botsford
& Robinson's Hellenic Hist., p. 115-121; 127-142. T. B.
Bury's Hist. of Greece, p. 216-229; 240-241; 259-269; 471-
472. The Tutorial Hist of Greece by W. J. Woodhouse, c. 18,
20 and 21).

C. *The Peloponnesian Wars* 460-445 *B. C. and* 431-421 *B. C.*

Owing to the ambitions of Athens to dominate the Ionians
and other neighboring peoples, Pericles launched a campaign
of alliances and conquests extending from Thessaly to Argos,
and from Euboea to Naupactus, Achaea and the chief islands
of the Ionian Sea.

The net results were as follows: (a) Athens established
alliances with Boeotia, Phocis and Locris, in spite of Sparta's
opposition. (b) In 456 B. C. Aegina was captured and made
tributary. (c) In 450 B. C. Athens failed in her attempt to
invade Corinth. (d) In 451 friendship between Athens and
Sparta was restored through the instrumentality of Cimon,
on the condition that Athenian alliance with Argos was dis-
solved. (e) In 447 B. C. the exiled Oligarchs of Thebes defeated the Athenians at Coronea, and reestablished the Boeotian League under Theban leadership. (f) In 445 B. C. the 30
years peace was signed and after the revolt of Euboea and
Megara, Sparta invaded Attica and Pericles sued for peace.
Athens lost all her continental holdings. (Sandford's Mediterranean World C. 13, P. 220).

The second Peloponnesian war (431-421 B. C.) like that of

the first arose through a general spirit of rebellion among the Greek city states against Athenian imperialism, Sparta being the chief enemy.

The net results were as follows: (a) In 435 B. C. war between Corcyra and Corinth, Corcyra being aided by Athens.

(b) In 432 B. C.

    (1) Athens blockaded Potidaea, because she refused to dismantle her Southern walls, and dismiss her Corinthian Magistrates.

    (2) Megara was excluded from Greek Markets, in order to reduce her to subjection.

    (3) The Peloponnesian League planned war against Athens and Boeotia. Phocis and Locris were to fight against Athens, Corcyra and a few Northern states.

(c) In 431 B. C.

    (1) Thebes attacked Plataea, and while a Peloponnesian army occupied Attica, the Athenian fleet raided Peloponnesus.

    (2) Pericles being unable to defend Attica adequately transferred the civil population every Spring to the area between the walls of Athens and the Peiraeus. In the meantime the Athenian fleet operated against Potidaea, the Peloponnesian coast and Corinthian commerce.

(d) In 428 B. C.

    (1) Mitylene and all the cities of Lesbos revolted.

    (2) A brutal massacre of Oligarchs took place at Corcyra.

(e) In 425 B. C.

    (1) A Laconian force at Pylos was captured and a fort was established through Demosthenes and Cleon.

    (2) Cythera and other stations were fortified against the Peloponnesians.

    (3) Amphipolis was captured by Brasidas a Spartan, who had instigated rebellion among the Athenian

allies, and after Brasdias and Cleon had been killed in battle (422 B. C.), Athens authorized Nicias to sue for peace. (Sandford's Mediterranean World C. 13, P. 220-221).

It is obvious from a study of the causes and effects of the Peloponnesian wars that

(a) The Greek states were envious of each other and

(b) The desire for power and expansion led to constant aggression and warfare among themselves.

(c) The condition of constant warfare between the city states was unfavourable for the production of philosophers.

Before passing on to consider my next proposition I would like to say that it is an accepted truth that the development of philosophical thought requires an environment which is free from disturbance and worries. The period commonly assigned to Greek philosophy (i.e. Thales to Aristotle) was exactly the opposite to one of peace and tranquility, and therefore it could not be expected to produce philosophy. The obstacles against the origin and development of Greek philosophy, were not only the frequency of civil wars; and the constant defense against Persian aggression; but also the threat of extermination from the Athenian government, its worst enemy.

D. PHILOSOPHY REQUIRES A SUITABLE ENVIRONMENT.

I must now add the following quotation which depicts this period. "For although the natural ills that beset mankind are many, we ourselves have added to them by wars and civil strife against one another, so that some have been unjustly put to death in their own cities, others driven into exile with their wives and children, and many have been compelled, for the sake of their daily bread, to die fighting against their own people, for the sake of the enemy". (Isocrates)

(Botsford & Robinson's Hellenic Hist., c. XIII. Couch's Hist. of Greece, c. XXII. Bury's Hist. of Greece, c. X. The Tutorial Hist. of Greece by W. J. Woodhouse, c. 27, 28 and 29).

[26]

CHAPTER III:

Greek Philosophy Was the Offspring of The Egyptian Mystery System.

1. The Egyptian Theory of Salvation Became the Purpose of Greek Philosophy.

THE earliest theory of salvation is the Egyptian theory. The Egyptian Mystery System had as its most important object, the deification of man, and taught that the soul of man if liberateu from its bodily fetters, could enable him to become godlike and see the Gods in this life and attain the beatific vision and hold communion with the Immortals (Ancient Mysteries, C. H. Vail, P. 25).

Plotinus defines this experience as the liberation of the mind from its finite consciousness, when it becomes one and is identified with the Infinite. This liberation was not only freedom of the soul from bodily impediments, but also from the wheel of reincarnation or rebirth. It involved a process of disciplines or purification both for the body and the soul. Since the Mystery System offered the salvation of the soul it also placed great emphasis upon its immortality. The Egyptian Mystery System, like the modern University, was the centre of organized culture, and candidates entered it as the leading source of ancient culture. According to Pietschmann, the Egyptian Mysteries had three grades of students (1) The Mortals i.e., probationary students who were being instructed, but who had not yet experienced the inner vision. (2) The Intelligences, i.e., those who had attained the inner vision, and had received mind or *nous* and (3) The Creators or Sons of Light, who had become identified with or united with the Light (i.e., true spiritual consciousness). W. Marsham Adams, in the "Book of the Master", has described those grades as the equivalents of Ini

[27]

tiation, Illumination and Perfection. For years they underwent disciplinary intellectual exercises, and bodily asceticism with intervals of tests and ordeals to determine their fitness to proceed to the more serious, solemn and awful process of actual Initiation.

Their education consisted not only in the cultivation of the ten virtues, which were made a condition to eternal happiness, but also of the seven Liberal Arts which were intended to liberate the soul. There was also admission to the Greater Mysteries, where an esoteric philosophy was taught to those who had demonstrated their proficiency. (Ancient Mysteries C. H. Vail P. 24-25). Grammar, Rhetoric, and Logic were disciplines of moral nature by means of which the irrational tendencies of a human being were purged away, and he was trained to become a living witness of the Divine Logos. Geometry and Arithmetic were sciences of transcendental space and numeration, the comprehension of which provided the key not only to the problems of one's being; but also to those physical ones, which are so baffling today, owing to our use of the inductive methods. Astronomy dealt with the knowledge and distribution of latent forces in man, and the destiny of individuals, races and nations. Music (or Harmony) meant the living practice of philosophy i.e., the adjustment of human life into harmony with God, until the personal soul became identified with God, when it would hear and participate in the music of the spheres. It was therapeutic, and was used by the Egyptian Priests in the cure of diseases. Such was the Egyptian theory of salvation, through which the individual was trained to become godlike while on earth, and at the same time qualified for everlasting happiness. This was accomplished through the efforts of the individual, through the cultivation of the Arts and Sciences on the one hand, and a life of virtue on the other. There was no mediator between man and his salvation, as we find in the Christian theory. Reference will again be made to these subjects, as part of the Curriculum of the Egyptian Mystery System.

Now that we have outlined the Egyptian theory of salvation and its purpose, let us examine Greek philosophy and its purpose in order to discover whether there is an agreement between the two systems, or not.

2. Circumstances of identity between the Egyptian and Greek Systems.

A. *The Indictment and Prosecution of Greek Philosophers.*

The indictment and prosecution of Greek philosophers is a circumstance which is familiar to us all. Several philosophers, one after another, were indicted by the Athenian Government, on the common charge of introducing strange divinities. Anaxagoras, Socrates, and Aristotle received similar indictments for a similar offence. The most famous of these was that against Socrates which reads as follows. "Socrates commits a crime by not believing in the Gods of the city, and by introducing other new divinities. He also commits a crime by corrupting the youth". Now, in order to find out what these new divinities were, we must go back to the popular opinion which Aristophanes (423 B. C.) in the Clouds, aroused against him. It runs as follows: "Socrates is an evildoer, who busies himself with investigating things beneath the earth and in the sky, and who makes the worse appear the better reason, and who teaches others these same things (Plato's Apology C. 1-10; Aristophanes' Frogs, 1071; Apology 18 B. C., 19 C. Apology 24 B).

It is clear then that Socrates offended the Athenian government simply because he pursued the study of astronomy and probably that of geology; and that the other philosophers were persecuted for the same reason. But the study of science was a required condition to membership in the Egyptian Mystery System, and its purpose was the liberation of the Soul from the ten bodily fetters, and if the Greek philosophers studied the sciences, then they were fulfilling a required condition to membership in the Egyptian Mystery Sys-

[29]

tem and its purpose; either through direct contact with Egypt or its schools or lodges outside its territory.

B. *A Life of Virtue was a Condition Required by the Egyptian Mysteries as Elsewhere Mentioned.*

The virtues were not mere abstractions or ethical sentiments, but were positive valours and virility of the soul. Temperance meant complete control of the passional nature. Fortitude meant such courage as would not allow adversity to turn us away from our goal. Prudence meant the deep insight that befits the faculty of Seership. Justice meant the unswerving righteousness of thought and action.

Furthermore, when we compare the two ethical systems, we discover that the greater includes the less, and that it also suggests the origin of the latter. In the Egyptian Mysteries the Neophyte was required to manifest the following soul attributes:-

(1) Control of thought and (2) Control of action, the combination of which, Plato called *Justice* (i.e., the unswerving righteousness of thought and action). (3) Steadfastness of purpose, which was equivalent to *Fortitude*. (4) Identity with spiritual life or the higher ideals, which was equivalent to *Temperance* an attribute attained when the individual had gained conquest over the passional nature. (5) Evidence of having a mission in life and (6) Evidence of a call to spiritual Orders or the Priesthood in the Mysteries: the combination of which was equivalent to *Prudence* or a deep insight and graveness that befitted the faculty of Seership.

Other requirements in the ethical system of the Egyptian Mysteries were:-

(7) Freedom from resentment, when under the experience of persecution and wrong. This was known as courage. (8) Confidence in the power of the master (as Teacher), and (9) Confidence in one's own ability to learn; both attributes being known as Fidelity. (10) Readiness or preparedness for initiation. There has always been this principle of the Ancient

Mysteries of Egypt: "When the pupil is ready, then the master will appear". This was equivalent to a condition of efficiency at all times for less than this pointed to a weakness.

It is now quite clear that Plato drew the four Cardinal virtues from the Egyptian ten; also that Greek philosophy is the offspring of the Egyptian Mystery System.

C. (i) *There was a Grand Lodge in Egypt which had associated Schools and Lodges in the ancient world.*

There were mystery schools, or what we would commonly call lodges in Greece and other lands, outside of Egypt, whose work was carried on according to the Osiriaca, the Grand Lodge of Egypt. Such schools have frequently been referred to as private or philosophic mysteries, and their founders were Initiates of the Egyptian Mysteries; the Ionian temple at Didyma; the lodge of Euclid at Megara; the lodge of Pythagoras at Crotona; and the Orphic temple at Delphi, with the schools of Plato and Aristotle. Consequently we make a mistake when we suppose that the so-called Greek philosophers formulated new doctrines of their own; for their philosophy had been handed down by the great Egyptian Hierophants through the Mysteries. (Ancient Mysteries C. H. Vail P. 59). In addition to the control of the mysteries, the Grand Lodge permitted an exchange of visits between the various lodges, in order to ensure the progress of the brethren in the secret science.

We are told in the Timaeus of Plato, that aspirants for mystical wisdom visited Egypt for initiation and were told by the priests of Sais, "that you Greeks are but children" in the Secret Doctrine, but were admitted to information enabling them to promote their spiritual advancement. Likewise, we are told by Jamblichus of a correspondence between Anebo and Porphyry, dealing with the fraternal relations, existing between the various schools or lodges of instructions in different lands, how their members visited, greeted and assisted one another in the secret science, the more advanced being obliged to afford assistance and instruction to their brethren in the inferior Orders. (Jamblichus: correspondence between Anebo and Porphyry) (Plato's Timaeus) (W. L. Wilmshurst on meaning of Masonry).

Having stated that the Grand Lodge of ancient mysteries was situated in Egypt, with jurisdiction over all lodges and schools of the ancient world, it now remains to show that such a Grand Lodge, did actually and physically exist. In doing so, two things are necessary: first, a description of the Egyptian temple, of which our modern mystery lodges (called by different names) are copies, and second, a description of the actual remains of the Grand and Sublime Lodge of Ancient Egypt.

C. (ii) *A description of the Egyptian temple.*

Here I quote two authorities on the Egyptian temple, the first, C. H. Vail, on Ancient Mysteries P. 159 who says "that the Egyptian temples were surrounded with pillars recording the number of the constellations and the signs of the Zodiac or the cycles of the planets. And each temple was supposed to be a microcosm or a symbol of the temple of the Universe or of the starry vault called temple". The next authority is Max Muller, who in his Egyptian Mythology P. 187-193, has described Egyptian temples as follows:-

"Egyptian temples were made of stone, the outer courts of mud bricks. Wide roads led to the temples for the convenience of processions, while the immediate entrance was lined with statues, consisting of sphinxes and other animals. The front wall formed two high tower like buildings, called pylons, before which stood two granite obelisks. Immediately behind the pylons came a large court where the congregation assembled and watched the sacrifices. Immediately next to the hall of the congregation, came the hall of priests, and immediately following the hall of the priests came the final chamber, called the Adytum, i.e., the Holy of Holies, which was entered only by the high Priest. This was the place of the shrine and the abode of the God. Each temple was a reproduction of the world. The ceilings were painted to represent the sky and the stars, while the floor was green and blue like the meadows. Ceremonial cleanliness was at all times imperative, and the people before entering the temple must carefully purify themselves in a nearby stream. In later times, this became a ceremony of sprinkling with holy water before entrance into the temple".

It is clear from the foregoing description that not only the modern masonic lodges, are copies of the Egyptian temple, but also the ancient ones, for there is complete identity in their internal decoration. But the minor or lower lodges including those outside of Egypt, must have had a governing body, and so now, I proceed to quote C. H. Vail, who in his Ancient Mysteries, pages 182 and 183, describes fully the location and remains of the famous Grand Lodge of Luxor, as follows:-

C. (iii) *The location of the Masonic Grand Lodge of Antiquity.*

"At a short distance from Danderah, now called Upper Egypt, is the most extraordinary group of architectural ruins presented in any part of the world, known as the Temples of the ancient city of Thebes. Thebes in its prime occupied a large area on both sides of the Nile. This city was the centre of a great commercial nation of Upper Egypt ages before Memphis was the capital of the second nation in Lower Egypt; and however grand the architectural monuments of the latter may have been those of the former surpassed them. The portrayal by pencil or brush can convey but a faint idea of the perfected city. As the city stands today, it is like a city of giants, who after a long conflict have been destroyed, leaving the ruins of their various temples, as the only proof of their existence

"The Temple of Luxor (it was in this temple that the Grand Lodge of Initiates always met), stands on a raised platform of brickwork covering more than two thousand feet in length and one thousand feet in breadth (note the oblong shape, which became the pattern for all lodges and churches in the ancient world). It is the one that interests the members of all Ancient Orders, especially so, all the members of those Orders that worshipped at the Shrine of the Secret Fire, more than perhaps any other, and stands on the eastern bank of the Nile. It is in a very ruined state; but records say the stupendous scale of its proportions almost takes away the sense of its incompleteness. Up to about a quarter of a century ago, the greater part of its columns in the interior and outer walls had been removed, after falling, for use elsewhere. This temple was founded by the Pharaoh Amenothis III, who constructed the southern part, including the heavy colonnade overlooking the river; but destruction unfortunately conceals this fact. The chief entrance to the Temple looked to the east; while the Holy Chambers at the upper end of the plain approached the Nile. As mighty as the Temple of Luxor was, it was exceeded in magnitude and grandeur by that of Carnak. The distance between these two great structures was a mile and a half. Along this avenue was a double row of Sphinxes, placed twelve feet apart, and the width of the avenue was sixty feet. When in perfect state this avenue presented the most extraordinary entrance that the world has ever seen. If we had the power to picture from the field of imagination the grand processions of Neophytes constantly passing through and taking part in the ceremonies of Initiation, we would be powerless to produce the grandeur of the surroundings, and the imposing sight of colour and magnificent trappings of those who took part. Neither can we produce the music that kept the vast number of people in steady marching order. Crude it might have been to the cultivated ear of the 20th century. But could not the palpitating strain sung by massed voices on the lapse of time, whose history launches the profoundest aspirations of the human heart, like the trend of a mighty river, because the grand currents of Universal Law, imparting the desire to that Shadowy Past, as it steps forth from the pages of history, dim with age? Egypt must have been, when these Temples were built, a martial nation for

records of her warlike deeds are perpetuated in deeply en-
graved tablets which even now, excite the admiration of the
best Judges of archaeological remains. She was also a highly
civilized nation, and of a nature that could bear the expendi-
ture which always attends the culture of the Arts. She surpassed in her astonishing architecture, all other nations that
have existed upon the earth."

I am fully convinced by these references and quotations that
an Egyptian Grand Lodge of Ancient Mysteries actually existed some five thousand years ago or more, on the banks
of the Nile in the city of Thebes, and that it was the only
Grand Lodge of the Ancient World whose ruins have been
found in Egypt, and that it was the governing body which
necessarily controlled the Ancient Mysteries together with the
philosophical Schools and minor Lodges wherever they hap-
pened to have been organized.

C. (iv) *The rebuilding of the temple of Delphi.*

The temple of Delphi was burnt down in 548 B. C. and
it was King Amasis of Egypt, who rebuilt it for the brethren,
by donating three times as much as was needed, in the sum
of one thousand talents, and 50,000 lbs. of alum. According
to information at hand, the temple had organized its members into an amphictyonic league for protection against political and other forms of violence; but they were too poor to
raise suffcent funds from the membership, and they decided
upon a public contribution from the citizens of Greece.

Accordingly they wandered throughout the land soliciting
aid, but failed in their efforts. Having decided to visit the
brethren in Egypt, they approached King Amasis, who as
Grand Master, unhesitatingly offered to rebuild the Temple,
and donated more than three times as much as was needed
for the purpose.

N.B. Here it would be well to note that

(1) The Greeks regarded the Temple of Delphi as a
    foreign institution, hence

[35]

(2) They were unsympathetic towards it and for the same reason destroyed it by fire.

(3) Clearly, the Temple of Delphi was a branch of the Egyptian Mystery System, projected in Greece.

Sandford's Mediterranean World p. 135; 139.

John Kendrick's Ancient Egypt Bk. II. P. 363.

3. The abolition of Greek Philosophy together with the Egyptian Mysteries.

From the conquest of Egypt by Alexander the Great, the Greeks, who were always attracted by the mysterious worship of the Nile-land, began to imitate the Egyptian religion in its entirety; and during the Roman occupation, the Egyptian religion spread not only to Italy: but throughout the Roman Empire, including Britanny.

This assimilation of the Egyptian religion was confined to the Gods of the Osirian cycle and the Graeco-Egyptian Serapis, and aimed at a close imitation of the ancient traditions of the Nile-land. Owing to the splendour of architecture, the hieroglyphs of the temples, the obelisks and sphinxes before the shrines, the linen vestments and the shaven heads and faces of the priests, the endless and obscure ritual, filled the Greeks with awe, and wonderful mysteries were consequently believed to have underlain these incomprehensibles, and the Egyptian religion stood in the way of the rising Christianity.

The success of the Egyptian religion was due no doubt, on the one hand to its conservatism; while on the other to the shadowy philosophical abstractions which constituted Graeco-Roman religion, so that the staunch faith of the Egyptians, together with their mysterious forms of worship, led to the universal conviction among the Ancients, that Egypt was not only the Holy Land but the Holiest of lands or countries, and that indeed, the Gods dwelt there.

The Nile became a centre for pilgrimages in the ancient world, and the pilgrims who went there and experienced the marvellous revelations and spiritual blessings which it afforded them, returned home with the conviction that the Nile was the home of the most profound religious knowledge.

The Greeks failed to imitate Egyptian conservatism and not only in Egyptian cities, with large Greek population, but in Europe, Egyptian divinities were corrupted with Greek and Asiatic names and mythologies and reduced to vague pantheistic personalities, so that Isis and Osiris had retained very little of their Egyptian origin. (Max Muller p. 241-43. Egyptian Mythology). Consequently, as they failed to advance Egyptian Philosophy, so they also failed to advance Egyptian religion.

During the first four centuries of the Christian era, the religion of Egypt continued unabated and uninterrupted, but after the Edict of Theodosius at the end of the fourth century A. D., ordering the close of Egyptian temples, Christianity began to spread more rapidly and both the religion of Egypt and that of Greece began to die. In the island of Philae, in the first cataract of the Nile, however, the Egyptian religion was continued by its inhabitants, the Blemmyans and Nobadians, who refused to accept Christianity and the Roman government fearing a rebellion, paid tribute to them as an appeasement.

During the sixth century A. D., however, Justinian issued a second edict which suppressed this remnant of Egyptian worshippers and propagated Christianity among the Nubians. With the death of the last priest, who could read and interpret "the writings of the words of the Gods" (the hieroglyphics) the Egyptian faith sank into oblivion. It was only in popular magic that some practices lingered on as traces of a faith that became a universal religion, or the survival of a statue of Isis and Horus, which were regarded as the Madonna and Child.

A sentiment of admiration and awe for this strangest of all religions still survived, but the information from classical writers concerning this faith has been incomplete. Napoleon's invasion of Egypt brought a revival of interest from the West to decipher her inscriptions and papyri with a view to an understanding and appreciation of this most ancient of civilizations.

(Mythology of Egypt by Max Muller C. XIII p. 241-245; The Mediterranean World by Sandford, p. 508, 548, 552-558, 568).

We learn the following facts from the above quotations:-
(i) The Egyptian Mysteries had become the Ancient World Religion, spreading throughout the Roman Empire and including Italy, Greece, Asia Minor, and various parts of Europe including Brittany. This continued under different names, long after Justinian's Edict of toleration granted to the Christians. (ii) Egypt was the Holy Land of the ancient world, that pilgrimages were made to that land because of the marvellous revelations and spiritual blessings which it afforded the ancient peoples, and because of the universal conviction among the Ancients that Egypt was the land of the Gods. (iii) The Edicts of Theodosius in the fourth century A. D,. and that of Justinian in the sixth century A. D. abolished alike not only the Mystery system of Egypt, but also its philosophical schools, located in Greece and elsewhere, outside Egypt.

(iv) The abolition of the Egyptian Mysteries was to create an opportunity for the adoption of Christianity. This was the problem: the Roman government felt that Egypt was now conquered in arms and reduced to her knees, but in order to make the conquest complete, it would be necessary to abolish the Mysteries which still controlled the religious mind of the ancient world. There must be a New World Religion to take the place of the Egyptian religion. This New Religion, which should take the place of the Mysteries, must be equally powerful and universal, and consequently everything possible must be done in order to promote its interests. This explains the rapid growth of Christianity following Justinian's Edict of toleration.

(v) Since the Edicts of Theodosius and Justinian abolished both the Mysteries of Egypt and the schools of Greek philosophy alike, it shows that the nature of the Egyptian Mysteries and Greek philosophy was identical and that Greek philosophy grew out of the Egyptian Mysteries.

4. How the African Continent gave its Culture to the Western World.

As mentioned elsewhere, the Egyptian Mysteries and the philosophical schools of Greece were closed by the edicts of Theodosius in the 4th century A. D. and that of Justinian in the 6th century A. D. (i.e., 529); and as a consequence, intellectual darkness spread over Christian Europe and the Graeco-Roman world for ten centuries; during which time, knowledge had disappeared. As stated elsewhere, the Greeks showed no creative powers, and were unable to improve upon the knowledge which they had received from the Egyptians (Hist. of Science by Sedgwick and Tyler p. 141; 153; Zeller's Hist. of Phil. Introduction p. 31).

During the Persian, Greek and Roman invasions, large numbers of Egyptians fled not only to the desert and mountain regions, but also to adjacent lands in Africa, Arabia and Asia Minor, where they lived, and secretly developed the teachings which belonged to their mystery system. In the 8th century A. D. the Moors, i.e., natives of Mauritania in North Africa, invaded Spain and took with them, the Egyptian culture which they had preserved. Knowledge in the ancient days was centralized i.e., it belonged to a common parent and system, i.e., the Wisdom Teaching or Mysteries of Egypt, which the Greeks used to call *Sophia*.

As such, the people of North Africa were the neighbours of the Egyptians, and became the custodians of Egyptian culture, which they spread through considerable portions of Africa, Asia Minor and Europe. During their occupation of Spain, the Moors displayed with considerable credit, the grandeur of African culture and civilization. The schools and libraries which they established became famous throughout the Mediaeval world; Science and learning were cultivated and taught; the schools of Cordova, Toledo, Seville and Saragossa attained such celebrity, that they, like their parent Egypt, attracted students from all parts of the Western world; and from them arose the most famous African professors that the

[39]

world has ever known, in medicine, surgery, astronomy and mathematics. But these people from North Africa did more than merely distinguish themselves in Spain. They were really the recognized custodians of African culture, to whom the world looked for enlightenment. Consequently, through the medium of the ancient Arabic language, philosophy and the various branches of science were disseminated: (a) all the so-called works of Aristotle in Metaphysics, moral philosophy and natural science (b) translations by Leonardo Pisano in Arabic mathematical science (c) translation by Gideo a Monk of Arezzo in musical notation. (Sedgwick and Tyler's Hist. of Science C. IX.)

In addition, the Moors kept up constant contact with mother Egypt: for they had established Caliphates not only at Baghdad and Cordova, but also at Cairo in Egypt. (Europe in the Middle Ages by Ault p. 216-219). Just here it would be well to mention that all the great leaders of the great religions of antiquity were Initiates of the Egyptian Mystery System: from Moses, who was an Egyptian Hierogrammat, down to Christ.

It should also be of interest to know that European scientists like Roger Bacon, Johann Kepler, Copernicus and others obtained their science through Arab or Berber sources. It is also noteworthy that throughout the Middle Ages, European knowledge of medicine came from these same sources.

(History of The Arabs, by Hitti pages 370, 629, 665 and 572).

(Philo; Esoteric Christianity by Annie Besant p. 107; 128-129; Ancient Mysteries by C. H. Vail p. 59; 61; 74-75; 109).

CHAPTER IV:

The Egyptians Educated the Greeks.
1. The Effects of the Persian Conquest.

A. *Immigration restrictions against the Greeks are removed and Egypt is thrown open to Greek research.*

Owing to the practice of piracy, in which the Ionians and Carians were active, the Egyptians were forced to make immigration laws restricting the immigration of the Greeks and punishing their infringement by capital punishment, i.e., the sacrifice of the victim. Before the time of Psammitichus, the Greeks were not allowed to go beyond the coast of Lower Egypt, but during his reign and that of Amasis, those conditions were modified. For the first time in Egyptian history Ionians and Carians were employed as Mercenaries in the Egyptian Army (670 B. C.), interpretation was organized through a body of interpreters, and the Greeks began to gain useful information concerning the culture of the Egyptians.

In addition to these changes, King Amasis removed the restrictions against the Greeks and permitted them to enter Egypt and settle in Naucratis. About this same time, i.e., the reign of Amasis, the Persians, through Cambyses invaded Egypt, and the whole country was thrown open to the researches of the Greeks.

B. *The Genesis of Greek Enlightenment.*

The Persian invasion, did not only provide the Greeks with ample research, but stimulated the creation of prose history in Ionia. Heretofore, the Greeks had little or no accurate knowledge of Egyptian culture: but their contact with Egypt resulted in the genesis of their enlightenment. (Ovid Fasti III 338; Herodotus Bk. II p. 113; Plutarch p. 380; Eratosthenes ap Strabo 801-802; Diogenes Bk. IX 49).

[41]

C. *Students from Ionia and the Islands of the Aegean visit Egypt for their Education.*

Just as in our modern times, countries like the United States, England, and France are attracting students from all parts of the world, on account of their leadership in culture; so was it in ancient times, Egypt was supreme in the leadership of civilization, and students from all parts, flocked to that land, seeking admission into her mysteries or wisdom system.

The immigration of Greeks to Egypt for the purpose of their education, began as a result of the Persian invasion (525 B. C.), and continued until the Greeks gained possession of that land and access to the Royal Library, through the conquest of Alexander the Great. Alexandria was converted into a Greek city, a centre of research and the capital of the newly created Greek empire, under the rule of Ptolemies. Egyptian culture survived and flourished, under the name and control of the Greeks, until the edicts of Theodosius in the 4th century A. D., and that of Justinian in the 6th century A. D., which closed the Mystery Temples and Schools, as elsewhere mentioned. (Ancient Egypt by John Kendrick Bk. II p. 55; Sandford's Mediterranean World p. 562; 570).

Concerning the fact that Egypt was the greatest education centre of the ancient world which was also visited by the Greeks, reference must again be made to Plato in the Timaeus who tells us that Greek aspirants to wisdom visited Egypt for initiation, and that the priests of Sais used to refer to them as children in the Mysteries.

As regards the visit of Greek students to Egypt for the purpose of their education, the following are mentioned simply to establish the fact that Egypt was regarded as the educational centre of the ancient world and that like the Jews, the Greeks also visited Egypt and received their education. (1) It is said that during the reign of Amasis, Thales who is said to have been born about 585 B. C., visited Egypt and was initiated by the Egyptian Priests into the Mystery System and science of the Egyptians. We are also told that during his residence in Egypt, he learnt astronomy, land surveying, mensuration, engineering and Egyptian Theology. (See Thales in Blackwell's source book of Philosophy; Zeller's Hist. of Phil.; Diogenes Laertius and Kendrick's Ancient Egypt).

(2) It is said that Pythagoras, a native of Samos, travelled frequently to Egypt for the purpose of his education. Like every aspirant, he had to secure the consent and favour of the Priests, and we are informed by Diogenes that a friendship existed between Polycrates of Samos and Amasis King of Egypt, that Polycrates gave Pythagoras letters of introduction to the King, who secured for him an introduction to the Priests; first to the Priest of Heliopolis, then to the Priest of Memphis, and lastly to the Priests of Thebes, to each of whom Pythagoras gave a silver goblet. (Herodotus Bk. III 124; Diogenes VIII 3; Pliny N. H., 36, 9; Antipho recorded by Porphyry).

We are also further informed through Herodotus, Jablonsk and Pliny, that after severe trials, including circumcision, had been imposed upon him by the Egyptian Priests, he was finally initiated into all their secrets. That he learnt the doctrine of metempsychosis; of which there was no trace before in the Greek religion; that his knowledge of medicine and strict system of dietetic rules, distinguished him as a product of Egypt, where medicine had attained its highest perfection; and that his attainments in geometry corresponded with the ascertained fact that Egypt was the birth place of that Science. In addition we have the statements of Plutarch, Demetrius and Antisthenes that Pythagoras founded the Science of Mathematics among the Greeks, and that he sacrificed to the Muses, when the Priests explained to him the properties of the right angled triangle. (Philarch de Repugn. Stoic 2 p. 1089; Demetrius; Antisthenes; Cicero de Natura Deorum III, 36). Pythagoras was also trained in music by the Egyptian priests. (Kendrick's Hist. of Ancient Egypt vol. I. p. 234).

(3) According to Diogenes Laertius and Herodotus, Democritus is said to have been born about 400 B. C. and to

have been a native of Abdera in Miletus. We are also told by Demetrius in his treatise on "People of the Same Name", and by Antisthenes in his treatise on "Succession", that Democritus travelled to Egypt for the purpose of his education and received the instruction of the Priests. We also learn from Diogenes and Herodotus that he spent five years under the instruction of the Egyptian Priests and that after the completion of his education, he wrote a treatise on the sacred characters of Meroe.

In this respect we further learn from Origen, that circumcision was compulsory, and one of the necessary conditions of initiation to a knowledge of the hieroglyphics and sciences of the Egyptians, and it is obvious that Democritus, in order to obtain such knowledge, must have submitted also to that rite. Origen, who was a native of Egypt wrote as follows:-

"Apud Aegyptios nullus aut geometrica studebat, aut astronomiae secreta remabatur, nisi circumcisione suscepta." (No one among the Egyptians, either studied geometry, or investigated the secrets of Astronomy, unless circumcision had been undertaken).

(4) Concerning Plato's travels we are told by Hermodorus that at the age of 28 Plato visited Euclid at Megara in company with other pupils of Socrates; and that for the next ten years he visited Cyrene, Italy and finally Egypt, where he received instruction from the Egyptian Priests.

(5) With regards to Socrates and Aristotle and the majority of pre-Socratic philosophers, history seems to be silent on the question of their travelling to Egypt like the few other students here mentioned, for the purpose of their education. It is enough to say, that in this case the exceptions have proved the rule, that all students, who had the means, went to Egypt to complete their education. The fact that history fails to supply a fuller account of this type of immigration, might be due to some or all of the following reasons:

(a) The immigration laws against the Greeks up to the time of King Amasis and the Persian Invasion, (b) Prose history was undeveloped among the Greeks during the period of their educational immigration to Egypt. (c) The Greek authorities persecuted and drove students of philosophy into hiding and consequently, (d) Students of the Mystery System concealed their movements.

Let us remember that Anaxagoras was indicted and imprisoned; that he escaped and fled to his home in Ionia, that Socrates was indicted, imprisoned and condemned to death; and that both Plato and Aristotle fled from Athens under great suspicion (William Turner's Hist. of Phil. p. 62; Plato's Phaedo; Zeller's Hist. of Phil. p. 84; 127; Roger's Hist. of Phil. p. 76; William Turner's Hist. of Phil. p. 126).

2. The Effects of the Conquest of Egypt by Alexander the Great.

A. *The Royal Library and Museum together with Temples and other Libraries are Looted.*

As elsewhere mentioned, it was an ancient custom of invading armies to loot libraries and temples in order to capture books and manuscripts, which were regarded as great treasures. A few instances would be enough to verify this custom: (a) we are informed that during the Persian Invasion beginning with Cambyses, the temples of Egypt were not only stripped of their gold and silver, but rifled for their ancient records. Every Egyptian Temple carried a secret library with secret manuscripts and books. (b) We are also informed that when Athens was captured by the Romans in 84 B. C. the library of books said to have belonged to Aristotle was also captured and taken to Rome. (William Turner's Hist. of Phil. p. 128; John Kendrick's Ancient Egypt vol. II p. 432).

Just as in the invasion of Egypt by the Persians, the invading armies stripped the temples of their gold, silver and sacred books; and just as in the capture of Athens by the Romans Sulla carried off the only library of books which he found; so it is to be expected of Alexander the Great, in his invasion of Egypt. One of the first things that he and his companions and armies would do, would be to search for the treasures of the land and capture them. These were kept in temples and libraries and consisted of gold and silver out of which the gods and ceremonial vessels were made, and sacred books and, manuscripts kept both in libraries and in the "Holy of Holies" of Temples.

It is my firm belief that this indeed was the great opportunity which Alexander gave Aristotle and enabled him and his pupils to carry off as many books as they wanted from the Royal Library and to convert it into a research centre. Apart from the Royal Library at Alexandria, there was also another famous library near by: The "Royal Library of Thebes"; "The Menephtheion", which was founded by Pharaoh, Setei. The Menephtheion was completed by Rameses II; but little occurs in history about this greatest of Egyptian Royal Libraries.

However, any invading army would first loot the Royal Library of Alexandria and then would turn their attention to the Menephtheion at Thebes. They would also visit the cities of Memphis and Heliopolis and likewise loot their libraries and temples. This was the ancient custom and certainly one of the ways in which the Greeks received their education from Egyptians. (Egyptian Mythology by Max Muller p. 187-189; 205; Diodorus 16, 51; Bunsen I p. 27; Ancient Egypt by John Kendrick vol. II 56; 432-433).

It is therefore an erroneous belief that the Greeks, on Egyptian soil, and through their own native ability, set up a great university at Alexandria and turned out great scholars. On the other hand, since it is a well known fact that Egypt was the land of temples and libraries, we can see how comparatively easy it was for the Greeks to strip other Egyptian libraries of their books in order to maintain the new Library at Alexandria, after it had been already looted by Aristotle and his pupils. The Greeks (i.e., Alexander the Great, Aristotle's school and the succeeding Ptolemies) converted the Royal Library of Alexandria into a research centre, by transferring

Aristotle's school and pupils from Athens to this great Egyptian Library, and therefore the students who studied there received instructions from Egyptian priests and teachers, until they died out. The difficulty of language and interpretation made it imperative for the Greeks to use Egyptian teachers.

The Greeks did not carry culture and learning to Egypt, but found it already there, and wisely settled in that country, in order to absorb as much as possible of its culture.

B. *The Royal Library of Thebes: The Menephtheion is described. It was also looted by invading armies.*

But when we read a brief sketch of the magnificence of the Theban Royal Library; The Menephtheion, we even see a better picture and are bound to admit that Egypt was the store house of ancient culture and that that culture was preserved in the form of literature stored away in her great libraries and temples. Great as the Royal Library of Alexandria might have been, we see in the Theban Royal Library something far more magnificent and far more representative of the true greatness of our Ancient Egypt.

On the left of the steps leading to the second court, there is still seen the pedestal of the enormous granite statue of Rameses; the largest, that ever existed in Egypt, according to Diodorus. Its height has been calculated at fifty-four feet, and its weight, at $887\frac{1}{4}$ tons; a marvel to the modern mind. The interior face of the wall of the pylon represents the wars of Rameses III. The Osiride pillars of the second court, are the monolithal figures, sixteen cubits in height, supplying the place of columns, and at the foot of the steps leading from the court to the next hall beyond, there were two sitting statues of the King. The head of one of these was of red granite, known by the name of "Young Memon", was taken away by Belzoni, and is now a principal ornament of the British Museum.

Beyond this are the remains of a hall 133 feet broad by 100 feet long, supported by 48 columns, twelve of which are

thirty-two feet in height and 21 feet in circumference. On
different parts of the columns, and the walls are represented
acts of homage by the king to the principal Deities of the
Theban Pantheon, and the gracious promises which they make
him in return.

In another sculpture the two chief Divinities of Egypt in-
vest him with the emblems of military and civil dominion,
i.e., the Scimitar, the Scourge and the Pedum. Beneath, the
twenty-three sons of Rameses appear in procession, bearing
the emblems of their respective high offices in the state, their
names being inscribed above them. Nine smaller apartments,
two of them still preserved, and supported by columns, lay behind the hall. On the jambs of the first of these apartments
are sculptured Thoth: the Inventor of Letters, and the Goddess
Saf, with the title of 'Lady of Letters'; and 'President of the
Hall of Books', accompanied the former with an emblem of
the sense of sight, and the latter of hearing.

There is no doubt that this is the "Sacred Library" which
Diodorus describes as the inscribed "Dispensary of the Mind".
It had an astronomical ceiling, in which the twelve Egyptian
months are represented, with an inscription from which important inferences have been drawn respecting the chronology
of the reign of Rameses III.

On the walls is a procession of priests, carrying the Sacred
Arts, and in the next apartment, the last that now remains, the
king is presenting offerings to the various Divinities. (Ancient
Egypt by J. Kendrick Bk. I p. 128-131. Report of French
Commission).

C. *Museum and the Library of Alexander were used as a
University.*

The Museum and Library of Alexandria were so famous in
ancient times, that we wonder why more information concerning this centre of learning, has not come down to us. A few
references to authoritative sources might no doubt help to en-
lighten us on this matter.

From Sedgwick's and Tyler's History of Science, chapter 5 pages 87-119, we learn that the subjugation of Egypt by Alexander the Great in 330 B. C. had checked the further development of Greek civilization on its native soil.

That after the death of Alexander the Great in 323 B. C., his vast empire was divided among his generals, and that Alexandria, the new Egyptian capital fell to Ptolemy. That the city, barely ten years old, soon became the centre of the learned world, and that by 300 B. C., the Museum (i.e., the seat of the Muses), was founded, and became a veritable university of Greek learning.

That to the Museum was attached a great library, with a dining hall and lecture rooms for professors, and this became a school of philosophers, mathematicians and astronomers. Here for the next 700 years, science had its chief abiding place.

Here however, it should be remembered that the above statement of Sedgwick and Tyler is misleading, since the Greeks did not carry a civilization of their own to Egypt, but on the contrary found a very highly developed Egyptian culture, the survival of which was maintained by the use of Egyptian Priests and Scholars as teachers.

D. *A Military Policy of the Greeks to Commandeer Information From the Egyptians was put in operation.*

One of the military policies adopted by the Greek military authorities at Alexandria was the issue of commands to the leading Egyptian Priests for information concerning the Egyptian history, philosophy and religion. As a custom this is no less ancient than modern, since it is also a custom in modern times for victorious armies to confer with the men of science of an invaded country, in order to discover whether or not, there is anything new in the field of science, which they might possess. We would recall how at the end of World War II, the American scientists conferred with the Japanese scientists at Tokio. Accordingly, we are told that Ptolemy I Soter, in order to elicit the secrets of Egyptian wisdom or mystery system, ordered Manetho, the High Priest of the temple of Isis at Sebennytus in Lower Egypt, to write the philosophy, and the history of the religion of the Egyptians.

Accordingly, Manetho published several volumes concerning these respective fields, and Ptolemy issued an order prohibiting the translation of these books which had to be kept on reserve in the Library, for instruction of the Greeks by the Egyptian Priests. Here it becomes quite clear that the first professors of the Alexandrine School were the Egyptian Priests, and that the Scholarchs and pupils of Aristotle's transferred school, received their training directly from the Egyptian Priests. It is also well to note that the chief text books of the Alexandrine School were Manetho's books.

We are told by Apollodorus from whom Syncellus drew his information, that Ptolemy II ordered Eratosthenes, the Cyrenean (i.e., a black man and native of Cyrene) and librarian of the Alexandrine Library, to write a chronology of the Theban Kings, and that Eratosthenes did so with the aid of the Egyptian Hierophants at Thebes (Ancient Egypt by John Kendrick vol. II p. 81; Apollodorus; Syncellus; Clinton, Fasti Hellenici, sub anno).

Furthermore, it became the custom during the Greek and Roman occupation to use the services of Egyptian Priests and Scholars, as professors at the Alexandrine School. We are told that during the reign of Theodosius (378-395 A. D.), the Egyptian Professor Horapollo wrote a system of the Egyptian hieroglyphics: The Hieroglyphica of Horapollo, which has been regarded as the best that has come down to modern times. We are also told that this professor taught not only at the Alexandrine School, but also at that of Constantinople.

(John Kendrick's Ancient Egypt Bk. I p. 242; Leeman's Amstelod, 1935 translated by Cory).

3. The Egyptians Were the First to Civilize the Greeks.

Greece was first civilized by colonies from Egypt, then from

Phoenicia and Thrace. These were under the government of wise men, who not only subdued the ferocity of an ignorant populace by civil institutions, but also cast about them the strong chain of religion and the fear of the gods. Whatever dogmas they had been taught in their respective countries, concerning things divine and human, they delivered to these newly formed societies, with the object of bringing them under the restraint of virtuous discipline. Phoroneus and Cecrops were Egyptians, Cadmus a Phoenician and Orpheus a Thracian, and each of them, through their colonies carried into Greece the religious and philosophical tenets of his respective country.

The practice of teaching the doctrines of religion to people under the guise of myths originated from the Egyptians and was adopted by the Phoenicians and Thracians, and subsequently introduced to the Greeks.

According to Strabo, it was not possible in ancient times to lead a promiscuous multitude to religion and virtue by philosophical harangues. This could be effected only by the aid of superstition, by prodigies and fables. The thunder bolt, the aegis, the trident, the spear, torches and snakes were the instruments made use of by the founders of States, to terrify the ignorant and vulgar into subjection. These references must speak for themselves.

Cheops and Cecrops were the names which the Greeks used for the Egyptian Khufu, who belonged to the 4th Dynasty of the Egyptians or the pyramid age, i.e., 2800 B. C.

(Strabo Bk. I; Brucker's Historia Critica Philosophiae with translation by Wm. Enfield: Bk. II p. 62).

4. Alexander Visits the Oracle of Ammon in the Oasis of Siwah.

No discussion on Alexander's invasion of Egypt would be complete without reference to his famous visit to the Oracle of Ammon, situated in the Oasis of Siwah. Alexander had placed a garrison in Pelusium, whence he marched through the desert along the eastern bank of the Nile to Heliopolis where he crossed the river to Memphis, where his fleet had been awaiting him, and where he was welcomed by the Egyptians and crowned as Pharaoh. Having sacrificed to Apis and other Gods, Alexander descended the Nile by the Canopic branch and set out on his journey to the Oracle of Ammon in the Oasis of Siwah. His route was along the coast of Libya, as far as Paraetonium, whence he marched through the desert to the Oasis of Siwah. What do we suppose was Alexander's motive for visiting the Temple of Ammon? Perhaps a brief description of the religious and economic importance of Heliopolis, Memphis, Thebes and Ammonium might help us to determine what it was.

In the first place these cities were strongholds of the Egyptian religion, where there were many rich temples, schools and Priests, and therefore were representative of the Egyptian religious life. In the second place these cities were centres of education, and after the Persian invasion, Greek students who travelled to Egypt for the purpose of their education, received their training from the Priests of one or all of these cities, as elsewhere mentioned.

When Pythagoras went to Egypt, he carried a letter of introduction from Polycrates of Samos to King Amasis, who in turn gave him letters of introduction to the Priests of Heliopolis, Memphis, and Thebes. As centres of education, the temples and libraries of these cities contained very valuable books; and in the third place, these regions had previously been captured by the Persians for the very fact of their wealth. This should explain why they included these districts in their Satrapy which paid them an enormous annual tribute amounting to 700 talents of gold, together with the produce of the fisheries of Lake Moeris which amounted to a talent a day, during the six months that the water flowed in from the Nile; and a third part of that sum, during the afflux. In addition Egypt furnished 120 thousand medicini of corn as rations for the Persian troops who were stationed in the White Fort of Memphis. The equivalent of this tribute was 170 thousand pounds sterling, and shows the underlying motive not only of the Persian invading armies, but also of all invading armies of antiquity. In the case of Alexander there is no exception.

According to history, the Persians were in occupation of Egypt, and Alexander having mustered superior forces, went there and drove them out and took possession himself. May I ask this question: was this a joke, or was there a motive? And if there was a motive, what else could it have been but that Alexander wanted the wealth in books, gold, silver, ivory, slaves, and tribute which the Persians were extorting from the unfortunate Egyptians?

In ancient times, the Oracle of Ammon at Siwah was the most celebrated, and Heliopolis, Memphis and Thebes were representatives of the best of Egyptian culture.

(John Kendrick's Ancient Egypt Book II P. 433-435; Diodorus 15, 16. Herodotus Book III P. 124; Diogenes Laertius Book VIII; Timaeus of Plato; Pliny N. H. XXXVI 9; Antiphon recorded by Porphyry).

CHAPTER V:

The Pre-Socratic Philosophers and the Teachings Ascribed to Them.

N. B.

It is absolutely necessary here in chapters V and Vı to mention the doctrines of the so called Greek philosophers in order to convince my readers of their Egyptian origin which is shown in the summaries of conclusions which follow these teachings. It is also necessary to mention them so as to serve the purpose of reference and to meet the convenience of readers.

1. The Earlier Ionian School.

This Group consisted of (i) Thales (ii) Anaximander and (iii) Anaximenes.

(i) *Thales*, supposed to have lived 620-546 B. C. and a native of Miletus, is credited by Aristotle, with teaching that—

(a) water is the source of all living things.

(b) all things are full of God.

Both history and tradition are silent as to how Thales arrived at his conclusions, except that Aristotle attempts to offer his opinion as a reason: that is that Thales must have been influenced by the consideration of the moisture of nutriment, and based his conclusion on a rationalistic interpretation of the myth of Oceanus. This however is regarded as mere conjecture on the part of Aristotle. (Turner's History of Philosophy, p. 34).

(ii) *Anaximander*, supposed to have been born 610 B. C. at Miletus, is credited with the teaching that, the origin of all things is "the Infinite", or the Unlimited (i.e., apeiron), or the Boundless.

The Apeiron is regarded as equivalent to the modern notion of space, and the mythological notion of chaos.

Both history and tradition are silent as to how **Anaximander** arrived at his conclusion: but here again we find Aristotle offering his opinion as a reason, i.e., that Anaximander must have supposed that change destroys matter, and that unless the substratum of change is limitless, change must at sometime cease. This opinion, is of course, mere conjecture, on the part of Aristotle. (Turner's History of Philosophy, p. 35-36).

(iii) *Anaximenes,* also a native of Miletus, and supposed to have died in 528 B. C., is credited with the teaching that all things originated from air.

Both history and tradition are silent as to how Anaximenes arrived at his conclusion; and all attempts to furnish a reason are regarded as mere conjecture. (Turner's History of Philosophy, p. 37-38).

2. Pythagoras.

Born in the Aegean Island of Samos, supposedly in 530 B. C.; the following doctrines have been attributed to Pythagoras:-

(i) *Transmigration, the immortality of the soul and salvation.*

This salvation is based upon certain beliefs concerning the soul. True life is not to be found here on earth, and what men call life is really death, and the body is the tomb of the soul.

Owing to the contamination caused by the soul's imprisonment in the body, it is forced to pass through an indefinite series of re-incarnations: from the body of one animal, to that of another, until it is purged from such contamination.

Salvation, in this sense, consists of the freedom of the soul from the "cycle of birth, death and rebirth", which is common to every soul, and which condition must remain until purification or purgation is completed.

Being liberated from the ten chains of the flesh, and also from successive re-incarnations, the soul now acquires her pristine perfection, and the eligibility to join the company of the Gods, with whom she dwells for ever.

This was the reward which the Pythagorean System offered its initiates.

(ii) *The doctrines of (a) Opposites, (b) the Summum Bonum, or Supreme Good, and (c) the process of purification.*

(a) THE UNION OF OPPOSITES creates harmony in the universe. This is true in the case of musical sounds, such as we find in the lyre: where the harmony produced is the result of the mean proportional relation between the length of the two middle strings to that of the two extremes. This is also true in natural phenomena, which are identified with number, whose elements consist of the odd and the even. The even is unlimited, because of its quality of unlimited divisibility, and the odd indicates limitation; while the product of both is the unit or harmony.

Similarly, do we obtain harmony in the union of positive and negative; male and female; material and immaterial; body and soul.

(b) THE SUMMUM BONUM OR SUPREME GOOD in man, is to become godlike. This is an attainment, or transformation which is the harmony resulting from a life of virtue. It consists in a harmonious relationship between the faculties of man, by means of which his lower nature becomes subordinated to his higher nature.

(c) THE PROCESS OF PURIFICATION
The harmony and purification of the soul is attained, not only by virtue, but also by other means, the most important among them being the cultiva-

[57]

tion of the intellect through the pursuit of scientific knowledge and strict bodily discipline.

In this process, music also held an important place. The Pythagoreans believed and taught that just as medicine is used to cure the body, so music must be used to cure the soul.

Here it might be appropriate to insert the doctrine of the "Three Lives", since it is also a method and means of purification:-

"Mankind is divided into three classes: Lovers of wealth; lovers of honour, and lovers of wisdom (i.e. philosophers); this last, being highest." According to Pythagoras, philosophy determined the purification, which led to the final salvation of the soul.

(iii) *The Cosmological Doctrine*

All things are numbers, that is to say not only every object, but the entire universe is an arrangement of numbers. This means that the characteristic of any object is the number by which it is represented.

(a) Since the universe consists of ten bodies, namely, the five stars, the earth and the counter earth, then the universe must be represented by the perfect number ten.

(b) Applied to the space around us, but called by Pythagoreans the Boundless or Unlimited, it must be taken to mean, the measuring out of this Boundless, into a balanced and harmonious universe, so that everything might receive its proper proportion of it. No more, no less.

(c) This arrangement seems to suggest the notion of forms capable of receiving a mathematical expression, i.e., a doctrine which later appeared in Plato, as the theory of Ideas.

(d) In the centre of the universe there is a central fire around which the heavenly bodies fixed in their spheres, revolve from West to East, while around all there is the peripheral fire.

This motion of the heavenly bodies is regulated in the velocity, and produces the harmony of the spheres.

(Roger's Students' History of Philosophy p. 14-22).

(Bakewell's Source Book of Philosophy) (Life and Tenets of Pythagoras).

(Ruddick's History of Philosophy) (Life and Tenets of Pythagoras).

(Fuller's History of Philosophy) (Life and Tenets of Pythagoras).

(Turner's History of Philosophy: p. 40-43).

(History of Ancient Egypt by John Kendrick vol. I p. 401-402)

(Plato's Phaedo, 85E).

(Aristotle's Metaphysics I 5; 985b, 24; and I 5; 986a, 23).

3. The Eleatic Philosophers.

The Eleatic Philosophers include (a) Xenophanes, (b) Parmenides, (c) Zeno and (d) Melissus. They deal with the problem of change, and are credited with introducing the notions of Being and Becoming. The term Eleatic is derived from Elea, a city in Southern Italy, where these men are said only to have visited.

(a) XENOPHANES

Born at Colophon, in Asia Minor, about 370 B. C., Xenophanes is credited with the following doctrines:-

(i) THE UNITY OF GOD

Men err when they ascribe their own characteristics to the gods: for God is all eye, all ear, and all intellect. Again, since there is no Becoming, and since Plurality depends upon Becoming, therefore there is no Plurality. Consequently all is one and one is all.

[59]

(ii) TEMPERANCE

Against the artificial culture of Greece, its luxuries, excess and fops; Xenophanes is credited with advocating Temperance i.e., plain living, simplicity, moderation, and pure thinking.

Roger's Students' History of Philosophy: p. 27-28.
Wm. Turner's History of Philosophy: p. 45-46.
Zeller's History of Philosophy: p. 58-60.

(b) PARMENIDES

Is said to have been born at Elea 540 B. C. and to have composed a poem concerning nature: *peri physeos,* which contains his doctrines.

A. THE POEM consists of three parts:-

(i) In part one, the Goddess of truth points out that there are two paths of knowledge: one leading to a knowledge of truth, and the other to a knowledge of the opinions of men.

(ii) In part two, the journey to truth is described and contains a metaphysical doctrine, and in part three, a cosmology of the apparent.

B. THE DOCTRINES are as follows:-

(i) *The Physical Doctrine.*

Though right reason (logos) holds that Being is one and immutable, the senses and common opinion (doxa) are convinced that plurality and change exist around us.

(ii) *The Doctrine of Truth.*

Truth consists of the knowledge that Being is, and that not-Being is not: and since not-Being is not, then Being is one and alone.

Consequently, Being is unproduced and unchangeable. It is impossible for Being to produce Being; for under such circumstances Being must exist before it begins to exist.

(iii) *The doctrine of the Cosmology of the Apparent.*

Here Parmenides simply repeats the Pythagorean doctrine of opposites:-

All things are composed of light or warmth, and of darkness or cold, and according to Aristotle, the former of these opposites corresponds to Being, while the latter to not-Being.

These opposites are equivalent to the male and female principles in the cosmos.

(iv) *The Doctrine of the Anthropology of the Apparent*:- The life of the soul, i.e., perception and reflexion, depends upon the blending of opposites, i.e., of the light-warm and the dark-cold principles, each of which stands in a physical relation to a corresponding principle in the cosmos.

(Zeller's History of Philosophy p. 60-62).
(Roger's Students' History of Philosophy p. 29-30).
(William Turner's History of Philosophy p. 47-48).
(B. D. Alexander's History of Philosophy p. 22-24).

(c) ZENO

Supposed to be born 490 B. C. at Elea was a pupil of Parmenides, according to Plato. (Parmenides 127B).

His doctrines were intended to be a contradiction of (i) Motion and (ii) Plurality and space.

(i) Arguments against motion:-

(a) A body, in order to move from one point to another, must move through an infinite number of spaces since magnitude is divisible ad infinitum.

(b) A body which is in one place is at rest. An arrow in its flight, is at each successive moment in one place therefore it is at rest.

(c) The race between Achilles and the tortoise, is intended to contradict the concept of motion. In such a race Achilles can never overtake the tortoise, because he must first reach the point at which the tortoise started; but in the meantime the tortoise will have gained more ground. Since Achilles must always reach first the position previously occupied by the tortoise, the tortoise must always keep ahead, at every point.

(ii) Arguments against Plurality and Space:-

    (a) If a measure of corn produces a sound, then each grain ought to produce a sound. (This argument is taken from Simplicus: but ascribed to Zeno.)

    (b) If Being exists in space, then space itself must exist in space, and the process will have to go on ad infinitum. (This argument is also taken from Simplicus.)

    (c) If magnitude exists, it must be infinitely great and infinitely small, at one and the same time, since it has an infinitude of parts which are indivisible. Therefore the idea of the manifold is contradictory.

(William Turner's History of Philosophy p. 49-50).
(Roger's Students' History of Philosophy p. 31-32).
(Zeller's History of Philosophy p. 63-64).

4. The Later Ionian School: (a) Heraclitus, (b) Anaxagoras, (c) Democritus.

(a) HERACLITUS

Believed to have been born B. C. 530, and to have died in 470 B. C. Heraclitus, a native of Ephesus, in Asia Minor, has been credited with the following doctrines:-

(i) THE DOCTRINE OF UNIVERSAL FLUX

There is no static Being, and no Unchanging element. Change is Lord of the Universe. The underlying element of the universe is Fire, and all things are changed for Fire, and Fire for all things.

    (a) The change is not at random; but uniform, orderly and cyclic. Thus the heavenly Fires are transmuted successively, into vapour, water and earth;

only to go through a similar process as they ascend again into Fire.

(b) It contains the elements both of the old and new, at any given moment in the process. Consequently, where night ends, there day begins; where summer begins, there spring ends; and where mortal life ends, there spiritual life begins.

(c) It also consists in the generation which results from the union of opposites (a doctrine, later tc be found in Plato and Socrates).

Hence we observe that the union of male and female produces organic life; and that sharp and and flat notes produce harmony.

(ii) THE THEORY OF KNOWLEDGE

Since sense-knowledge, or knowledge derived from the senses is illusion, it must be avoided, and true knowledge sought for in the perception of the underlying unity of the various opposites.

This is possible for man, who is part of the all comprehending Fire, which underlies the Universe.

But in the doctrine of the upward and downward paths, true knowledge comes from the upward path which leads to the eternal Fire; whereas folly and death are the result of following the downward path.

(iii) THE DOCTRINE OF THE *LOGOS*

That the hidden harmony of nature ever reproduces concord from oppositions, that the divine law (*dikē*) or universal reason (*logos*) rules all things; and that the primitive essence recomposes itself anew in all things according to fixed laws, and is again restored by them.

(Zeller's History of Philosophy p. 68).
(A. B. Turner's History of Philosophy p. 66-77).
(Zeller's History of Philosophy p. 66-71).
(William Turner's History of Philosophy p. 53-58).

(b) THE LIFE AND TEACHINGS OF ANAXAGORAS

Anaxagoras, a native of Clazomenae, in Ionia, is supposed to have been born in 500 B. C. Like all the other philosophers, nothing is known about his early life and education. He comes into history through a visit to Athens, where he met and made the friendship of Pericles, and where he was charged with impiety. He however escaped from prison and fled back to his home in Ionia where he died in 430 B. C.

His doctrines included the following:-

(i) *Nous* i.e., mind alone is self-moved, and is the cause of motion in everything in the universe, and has supreme power over all things. (William Turner's History of Philosophy, p. 63); (Zeller's Hist. of Phil. p. 85; 86).

(ii) Sensation is produced by the stimulation of opposites. We experience the sensation of cold, because of the heat in us, and we experience a sweet taste because of the sour in us. (Wm. Turner's Hist. of Phil. p. 64; Theophrastus: de Sensu, Fragment 27: Zeller's Hist. of Phil. p. 86).

N. B.

These doctrines will be treated elsewhere, as regards their source and authorship.

(c) THE LIFE AND TEACHINGS OF DEMOCRITUS

(1) HIS LIFE

Democritus (420-316 B. C.) is said to have been the son of Hegesistratus, and also a native of Abdera, a city at Miletus, an island in the Aegean.

Both Aristotle and Theophrastus have regarded Leucippus as the founder of atomism, in spite of the fact that his existence is doubted. Like all the other Greek philosophers, nothing seems to be known about his early life and training. However he enters history as a magician and sorcerer.

(Burnet, op. cit. p. 350; Wm. Turner's Hist. of Phil. p. 65).

(2) HIS DOCTRINES

The name of Democritus has been associated with the following doctrines, summarized as atomism in his explanation of (i) the nature of the atoms, and their behavior in relation to the phenomena of (ii) creation (iii) life and death and (iv) sensation and knowledge

- (i) *The Description of the Atom*
  - (a) *The world-stuff.* The atom is explained as a colorless, transparent and homogeneous powder, consisting of an infinite number of particles.
  - (b) *Their Qualities*: The atom is described as full or solid, invisible, indestructible, uncreated and capable self-motion. The atoms differ in shape, order, position, quantity and weight.
  - (c) *The Identity of the Atom with Reality*: Every atom is equivalent to "that which is (i.e. *To on*); and the void is equivalent to "that which is not" (i.e., το *mē on*). Reality is the movement of "that which is," within that-which is not.

- (ii) *The Atom in Creation.*
  Owing to the difference in size, weight and mobility, and in particular to necessity, there is a resultant motion, by means of which the atoms combine themselves for the formation of the organic and inorganic worlds.

- (iii) *The Atoms in the Phenomena of Life and Death.*

What we commonly call life and death, are
due to a change in the arrangement of the
atoms. When they are arranged in a certain
way, life emerges; but when that arrangement
is changed to another way, then death is the
result.

In death, the personality disappears, the
senses also disappear; but the atoms live on for
ever. The heavier atoms descend to the earth:
but the soul atoms, which are composed of fire,
ascend to the celestial regions, whence they
came.

(iv) *The Atom in Sensation and Knowledge*

    (a) The Mind or Soul is composed of fire
atoms, which are the finest, the smoothest,
and the most mobile. These fire atoms are
distributed throughout the whole universe;
and in all animate things, and especially
in the human body, where they are found
in the largest numbers.

    (b) External objects constantly give off ema-
nations or minute images of themselves.
These in turn impress themselves upon
our senses, which set in motion our Soul
atoms, and thereby create Sensation and
Knowledge.

(Diogenes Laertius Book IX p. 443-455).
(Wm. Turner's History of Philosophy p. 65-70).
(Roger's Students History of Philosophy p. 40-42).
(Zeller's History of Philosophy p. 76-83).
(B. D. Alexander's History of Philosophy p. 37-41).

5. Summary of Conclusions Concerning the Pre-Socratic
Philosophers and the History of the Four Qualities
and Four Elements.

I. The early Ionic philosophers have been given the credit

of teaching the following doctrines (a) Thales, that all things originated from water, (b) Anaximander, that all things originated from Primitive matter, i.e., the boundless (to apeiron), and (c) Anaximenes, that all things get their life from air. But these ideas were not new at the time when these men are supposed to have lived, i.e., between the sixth and fifth centuries B. C. The creation story, found in the book of Genesis, speaks of the elements of water, air and earth as the cosmic ingredients of the chaos out of which creation gradually developed. The date of the Pentateuch is placed at the eighth century B. C.; but the view of the Mosaic authorship of Genesis takes us still further back into antiquity, and many centuries before the time of the Ionian philosophers. We are told not only by the bible, but also by the historian Philo, that Moses was an Initiate of the Egyptian Mysteries and became a Hierogrammat; learned in all the wisdom of the Egyptian people. This was only possible by proper initiation and gradual advancement, when evidence of fitness was demonstrated by the Neophyte. The Egyptian name of Moses was given to all candidates at their baptism, and meant "saved by water".

The Exodus of the Israelites appears to have occurred in the 21st Egyptian Dynasty, i.e., 1100 B. C. in the reign of Bocchoris under the leadership of Moses, whose creation story of Genesis is clearly of Egyptian origin. It is clear that the early Ionic Philosophers drew their teachings from Egyptian sources.

(Chaeremon: Jos. C. Apion I, 32; Philo; Ancient Mysteries C. H. Vail p. 61; John Kendrick's Ancient Egypt vol. 2 p. 268-270; 303; See also Dr. Hasting's Bible Dictionary, on authorship and date of Pentateuch).

II. In the case of the Eleatic philosophers, history regards Zenophanes as a Satirist, not a philosopher, and Zeno as paradoxical concerning his treatment of the problems of plurality, space and motion, which ultimately leads to a reductio ad absurdum. Parmenides introduced no new teaching when he spoke of Being (*To on*) as that which exists; and Non-Being (TO *mē on*) as that which does not exist. He only reemphasized the doctrine of opposites as a principle of nature: a doctrine taught not only by the Pythagoreans, but also the Athenian philosophers, chiefly Socrates. But the doctrine of opposites owes its origin to the Egyptian Mysteries which take us back to 4000 B. C. when it was demonstrated not only by double pillars in front of temples, but also by the pairs of Gods in the Mystery System, representing male and female, positive and negative principles of nature. It is also clear that the Eleatic Philosophers drew their teachings from Egyptian sources.

(Plato Phaedo; Memphite Theology: Intellectual Adventure of Primitive Man by Frankfort p. 55; 66-67; 51-60. Plutarch: Isis et Osiris, p. 364C; 355A; 371B; 868, Ancient Egypt: John Kendrick vol. I p. 339).

III. The later Ionic philosophers have been given credit for the following doctrines:

(1) Heraclitus, (a) that the world was produced by fire through a process of transmutation, and (b) since all things originate from fire, then Fire is the *Logos*: The Creator.

(2) Anaxagoras (a) the *Nous* or mind is the source of motion or life in the universe and that sensation is produced by the stimulation of opposites.

(3) Democritus (a) that atoms under-lie all material things, and (b) that the phenomena of life and death are merely changes in the mixture of the atoms, so that the atoms never die, because they are immortal.

These doctrines were by no means produced by the late Ionic philosophers, but could be shown to have originated from the Egyptian Mystery System. The Egyptians were fire worshippers, because they believed that fire was the creator of the universe, and built their great pyramids (*pyr=fire*) in order to worship the God of Fire, and the pyramid age goes back to something like 3300 B. C., several thousands of years before the Greeks were said to have come into the Mediterranean area.

According to Jamblichus the Egyptian God Ptah was the God of order and form in creation, an Intellectual Principle. This God was also recognized as the Divine Artificer who fashioned the universe out of fire.

Rosellini: mon del sults; John Kendrick's Ancient Egypt vol. I p. 318.

Furthermore, Swinburne Clymer in his Philosophy of Fire p. 18 has made the following statement "The study of the Mysteries of Isis and Osiris (Egyptian Goddess and God) quickly proves to the student that it was a pure Fire Philosophy. Zoroaster carried those mysteries into Greece, while Orpheus carried them into Thrace. In each of these places, these Egyptian mysteries assumed the names of different Gods in order to be adapted to local conditions. Hence in Asia they took the form of Mithra: in Samothrace, the form of the Mother of the Gods; in Boeotia, the form of Bacchus; in Crete, the form of Jupiter; in Athens, the forms of Ceres and Proserpine.

The most noted of these Egyptian imitations were the Orphic, Bacchic, Eleusinian, Samothracian, and Mithraic. All of these Fire Worshippers, believed that the universe originated from Fire, and they lived at a time which antedated the time of the late Ionic philosophers by thousands of years.

The other doctrines of the later Ionic philosophers together with those of Socrates, Plato and Aristotle will be treated under Summaries of Socrates, Plato and Aristotle and in Chapter VIII, and will include (1) Opposites (2) The *nous* or mind (3) The *Logos*, (4) The Atom, (5) The Theory of Ideas, (6) The Unmoved Mover, (7) Immortality.

IV. *The Greek Philosophers practised plagiarism.*

The teachings of Pythagoras seem to have been so comprehensive that nearly all his successors embraced and taught a

portion of his doctrine, which we are told he obtained by
frequent visits which he made to Egypt for the purpose of his
education. Two things are at once obvious, (1) that the Greek
philosophers practiced plagiarism and did not teach anything
new and (2) the source of their teachings was the Egyptian
Mystery System, either directly through contact with Egypt, or
indirectly through Pythagoras or tradition. These facts can
now be further demonstrated by an outline of the doctrines of
Pythagoras, with the names of philosophers who repeated his
doctrines:

1. *The Doctrine of Opposites*: the unit of number is composed both of odd and even elements; of the finite and infinite; and of the positive and negative. In this connection, we
find (a) Heraclitus suggesting fire to be the source of creation, by means of the principle of strife which separates phenomena; and harmony which restores them to their original
source. (William Turner's History of Philosophy p. 55; Zeller's Hist. of Phil. p. 67-68). (b) Parmenides, suggesting Being as existent and Non-Being as non-existent (Zeller's Hist. of
Phil. p. 61; Turner's Hist. of Phil. p. 48). (c) Socrates, attempting to prove the immortality of the Soul by the doctrine
of opposites (Plato Phaedo). (d) Plato, attempting to explain
nature, used the Theory of Ideas which he based upon the principle of opposites. Consequently the Idea is true reality, i.e.,
Being (*To on*); hence the concept is real; but the thing which
is known by the concept is unreal. The noumen is real and
perfect; but the phenomenon is unreal and imperfect (Parmenides 132D; Aristotle Meta 16, 987b9). (e) Aristotle in
attempting to establish the existence of God, describes the
divine attributes in terms of opposites. God is the First Mover
that is unmoved (*proton kinoûn akineton*). Hence, we have
a combination of motion and rest, as the attributes of Deity
and Nature. (Aristotle's physics VIII 5, 256a; II 1; 192b 14;
II 8, 199; de caelo I 4, 271a; Wm. Turner's Hist. of Phil. p.
141).

2. *The Doctrine of Harmony,* as a union of opposites, after being expounded by Pythagoras, appears also in the systems of (a) Heraclitus, who explains the phenomena of nature as passing successively through their opposites; (b) Socrates, who also defines harmony as the union of opposites; (c) Plato, who defines the harmony of the soul as the proper subordination of its parts, i.e., the higher and lower natures. (Turner's Hist. of Phil. p. 41; 56; Zeller's Hist. of Phil. p. 51; 69; Plato Phaedo C 15; Plato Republic); also (d) Aristotle, who defines the soul as a harmony in his de animo I. 2.

3. *The Central and Peripheral Fires.* Here Pythagoras attempts to show that fire under-lies creation, and this same notion is expressed by (a) Heraclitus, who speaks of the origin of the universe through the transformation of fire. Then we have (b) Anaxagoras (c) Democritus (d) Socrates and (e) Plato, each using the term mind (*nous*) as responsible for creation. Anaxagoras and Socrates who speak directly of mind (*nous*) as an Intelligence and purpose behind nature; while Democritus and Plato speak of mind (*nous*) indirectly as the World Soul, but further describe it as being composed of fire atoms floating throughout space. Clearly then, Mind (*nous*), no matter what other name or function we give it, is fire, since it is composed of fire atoms; and fire according to Pythagoras underlies creation. (Wm. Turner's Hist. of Phil. p. 42, 55, 63, 82; Zeller's Hist. of Phil. p. 53, 67, 76-83; Aristotle: Metaphysics I, 3, 984b, 17; Diogenes Laertius: Bk. X. p. 443-453; Xenophon Memorabilia I, 4, 2; Plato Timaeus: 30, 35; Roger's Student Hist. of Phil. p. 40-42; B. D. Alexander's Hist. of Phil. p. 43).

4. *Immortality of the Soul.* According to Pythagoras, the doctrine of the immortality of the Soul is implied in the doctrine of the Transmigration of the Soul:-

A. Socrates: The purpose of philosophy is the salvation of the Soul, whereby it feeds upon the truth congenial to its divine nature and thus escapes from the wheel of rebirth, and

[71]

finally attains the consummation of unity with God. (Zeller's
Hist. of Phil. p. 50-56; Roger's Hist. of Phil. p. 29 and 60;
William Turner's Hist. of Phil. p. 41 and 48).

B. Plato's doctrines (1) Transmigration and (2) Recollection: (1) Transmigration: the souls of men go to the place of
reward or punishment, and after one thousand years they are
permitted to choose a new lot of life. He who has thrice
chosen the higher life, gains after three thousand years, the
home of the Gods in the kingdom of thought. Others wander
about for thousands of years in various bodies; and many are
destined to pursue their earthly life in lower animal forms. It
is necessary to point out that in this doctrine of Transmigration, Plato describes the judgement scene in the Egyptian
Book of the Dead. (2) Recollection: although the sense per-
ceived world cannot lead us to a knowledge of Ideas, yet it
reminds us of the Ideas which we saw in a previous existence.

(The allegory of the Subterranean Cavern; Plato's Republic
C. X; The Allegory of the slave boy; Plato's Meno; Timaeus
of Plato: 31B, 33B; 38E; The Phaedo of Plato: C 15; 29;
57; Wm. Turner's Hist. of Phil. P. 105-112; B. D. Alexander's
Hist. of Phil. p. 55; 152-153).

5. *Summum Bonum*

According to Pythagoras, the supreme good in man is to become godlike. This transformation is to be accomplished by
virtue which is a union of opposites in man's faculties, i.e., the
subordination of man's lower nature to his higher nature.
(Zeller's Hist. of Phil. p. 43). But the precise purpose of the
Egyptian Mysteries was to make a man godlike by the puri-
ficatory agencies of education and virtue. Consequently it is
clear that Pythagoras obtained this doctrine directly from the
Egyptian Mysteries. Hence it also follows that philosophers
who have taught this doctrine, must have obtained it, either
directly from the Egyptian Mysteries, or indirectly, through
the teachings of Pythagoras. (According to Salust, Deification
or becoming godlike was the purpose of the Egyptian Mys-

[72]

teries, and according to C. H. Vail in his Ancient Mysteries, the Egyptian Summum Bonum consisted of five stages, during which the Neophyte developed from a good man into a triumphant Master, attaining the highest spiritual consciousness by means of casting off the ten bodily fetters and becoming an adept like Horus or Buddha or Christ).

The philosophers, besides Pythagoras, who are given credit with having taught the doctrine of the Supreme Good, are (a) Socrates, who defined it as an attainment in which man becomes godlike, through self-denial and the cultivation of the mind. (Xenophon Memorabilia I, 5, 4,) (b) Plato who defined it as happiness which is the attainment of the Idea of the Good, which is God. (Plato: Symposium 204E; Plato: Republic IV, 441, 443; Plato: Phaedo 64 sqq; Plato: Theaetetus 176 A). (c) Aristotle; who defined it as happiness which is based upon reason and which includes all the gifts of fortune. It should be noted however that Aristotle's definition of the Supreme Good marks the first departure from the concept of the Summum Bonum of the Egyptian Mysteries; and the same thing is true of the Hedonists, who defined it as pleasure. (Wm. Turner's Hist. of Phil. p. 153. Aristotle Ethics, Nic I, 6, 1097; Aristotle Ethics, Nic I, 9, 1099a, 31) The conception of a Supreme Good is Egyptian, from which source Pythagoras and other philosophers obtained the doctrine.

V. *SUMMARY OF CONCLUSIONS CONCERNING DEMOCRITUS*

Because of the importance of the doctrine of the atom, and the great suspicion of his great number of books like that of Aristotle, Democritus is treated separately, like each of the Athenian philosophers.

1. *HIS LIFE:*

The same thing might be said of Democritus as might be said of any of the men who were called Greek philosophers: nothing appears to be known about his early life and training. However he comes into history attracting public attention, as a sorcerer and magician. (Turner's Hist. of Phil. p. 65).

2. *HIS DOCTRINES AND AUTHORSHIP*:

(i) *Authorship*: The authorship of the doctrine of the atom is doubtful, from the standpoint or view of certain modern writers. The names of the Ionians Leucippus and Democritus have been associated with this doctrine, which according to the opinion of Aristotle and Theophrastus, originated through Leucippus, but was developed by Democritus.

As a matter of fact, the Ionians doubted the existence of Leucippus because he was unknown to them; and it seems proper that the opinion of the Ionians should receive credence rather than that of Aristotle and Theophrastus, who were Athenians, and who were compiling philosophy in the interest of their movement.

(Burnet op. cit. p. 350; Turner's Hist. of Phil. p. 65).

(ii) *The doctrine concerning the Atom is eclectic.*
The doctrine of the atom as explained by Democritus, is eclectic, and represents one of the many forms in which the ancient doctrine of opposites has been expressed. The Pythagoreans expressed it by the elements of number: odd and even.

Parmenides being unfamiliar with the law of generation, denied the existence of one opposite (not-Being), in order to affirm the existence of the other (being).

Socrates, being more acquainted with the law of generation than Parmenides, expressed it in several pairs of opposites, in an effort to prove the immortality of the soul: hence he spoke of unity and duality; of division and composition; of life and death.

In like manner Democritus expressed the doctrine of opposites, when he described Reality by the life of the atom, i.e., a movement of "that which is" (*To on*) within "that which is not" (το *mē on*).

The original source of this doctrine however, is the philosophy of the Mystery System of Egypt where we find the male and female principles of nature symbolized by (a) Osiris and Isis: the Egyptian God and Goddess, and (b) the Gods Horus and Seth, symbolizing a world in static equilibrium of conflicting forces, as they contend for dominion over Egypt.

(Memphite Theology; Kingship and the Gods by Frankfort C. 3, p. 25-26; 35; Herodotus I, 6-26; Ancient Egypt by John Kendrick Bk. I p. 339; Egyptian Religion by Frankfort, p. 64, 73 and 88; Zeller's Hist. of Phil. p. 61; Wm. Turner's Hist. of Phil. p. 41; Plato Phaedo C. 15, 16, 49).

The doctrine and philosophy of opposites is further demonstrated by the Egyptian Creation story, in which Order came out of Chaos and which was represented by four pairs of opposites i.e., male and female gods.

(a) Nun and Naunet i.e., primeval Matter and Space.
(b) Huk and Hauket i.e., Illimitable and the Boundless.
(c) Huh and Hauhet, i.e., Darkness and Obscurity.
(d) Amon and Amaunet, i.e., the hidden and concealed ones (the Air, Wind).

Clearly the doctrine of opposites was a basic philosophy of the Egyptians, being connected with not only the Gods of their Mystery dramas, but with their Cosmology, and since this connection makes the doctrine one of the earliest in the development of Egyptian thought, it antedates the reign of Menes, and means that the Egyptians were familiar with it before 3000 B. C.

Under these circumstances and in consequence of these facts, the Egyptian Mystery System was the source of the doctrines

(a) of the atom and (b) of opposites. Leucippus and Democritus taught nothing new and must have obtained their knowledge of the doctrines from the Egyptians, directly or indirectly.

(iii) *The Doctrines of the universal distribution of fire atoms, and their emanation from external objects are derived from Magic:-*

These doctrines are magical and express the magical principle "that the qualities of animals or things are distributed throughout all their parts." (Dr. Frazer's Golden Bough). Consequently within the universe contact is established between objects through emanations, and in the case of human beings, the result might be sensation or cognition; healing or contagion.

This principle is demonstrated not only by the cures such as were affected by the garment of Christ, and the handkerchiefs of St. Paul: but also by the modern scientific and medical practice of the preventive measure of quarantine. It must be remembered that magic was part of the education of the Egyptian priests: for the religious rites and ceremonies of the Egyptians were magical; and the priests were the custodians of the knowledge.

(iv) A fourth point is the fact that in the history and compilation of Greek philosophy by Aristotle and his followers, there are only two men whose names are associated with the authorship of an extraordinary number of scientific books; and the names of these men are Democritus himself and Aristotle.

(Diogenes Laertius Bk. 9 p. 445-461; Bk. 5 p. 465-467).

(v) A fifth point which deserves important mention is the fact that in the history and compilation of

Greek philosophy by Aristotle and his followers, it has been discovered that wherever there has been the possession of a large collection of scientific books, there has also been direct or indirect association with Alexander the Great.

(vi) The association between Democritus and Alexander the Great is seen through the Democritean Circle; a succession of Teachers and students, from a common original Teacher:- Democritus (420-316 B. C.) is said to have taught Metrodorus of Chios, who in turn is said to have taught Anaxarchus, who is said to have flourished at the time of the 110th Olympiad (340-337 B. C.), and to have accompanied Alexander the Great on his campaign against Egypt 333 B. C.

Here, it is easy to see the tie between Democritus and Anaxarchus for these men were all Ionians, and members of the same school and were alive at the time of Alexander's Conquest of Egypt. (Zeller's Hist. of Phil. p. 83; Diogenes Laertius Bk. 2, p. 471).

On the other hand, Aristotle's contact with Alexander the Great is well known, since he was a tutor of the young prince, at the Macedonian palace. Roger's Student Hist. of Phil. p. 104).

(vii) *Circumstantial evidence points to the fact that the books of Democritus were not written by him, nor did they contain his teachings. This is so, for the following reasons:-*

(a) Leucippus, whom the Ionians did not know, and whose existence has been questioned, has been given credit by Aristotle for the origin of the doctrine of the atom. (Zeller's Hist. of Phil. p. 77; Burnet, op. cit. p. 350) (Wm. Turner's Hist. of Phil. P. 65; Diogenes Bk. X, 13).

(b) Apart from what was written on the Atom, the name of Democritus is associated with a large list of books, dealing with over sixty different subjects, and covering all the branches of science known to the ancient world. In addition to this vast field of knowledge, the list also contains books on Military Science, Law and Magic. Clearly, the accumulation of such a vast range of knowledge, by a single individual, written in a single lifetime is impossible both physically and mentally. The method among the ancients of imparting knowledge was by gradual stages, followed by evidence of proficiency, which in turn was also followed by initiations, which marked every step in the progress of the Neophyte.

The progress of training was slow and no Neophyte could accomplish such knowledge in his life time as took the Egyptians over five thousand years to accumulate. These human limitations are as true today as they were among the ancients; for our great scientists of the Modern World are specialists only in single subjects.

(c) The question now remains: how did Democritus accumulate those books if he did not write them? We believe we have the answer because it has been noticed in the history of Greek philosophy that (a) wherever a Greek philosopher has had association, direct or indirect, with Alexander the Great, there was also the possession of a large collection of scientific books, and (b) this is true in the cases of Democritus and Aristotle. (c) Anaxarchus and Democritus were Ionians, who belonged to the same school and (d) Anaxarchus accompanied Alexander the Great on his campaign against Egypt. (The indirect association between Democritus and Alexander the Great now becomes obvious.) (e) It follows that since Alexander's conquest of Egypt had brought the Greeks their long hoped for opportunity, i.e., access to the Egyptian Library and Museum, we would naturally expect Alexander and his friends, and the invading armies to have helped themselves with the Egyptian books. We would also expect Anaxarchus upon his return to Ionia, to have sold, at least a portion of his loot, to Democritus, (nor do we expect Aristotle and Theophrastus to relate these facts to us), since under the rules of the Mysteries, knowledge (spoken or written,) could be diffused only by brethren among brethren. This we believe is the way Democritus came to possess such a large number of scientific books.

Again it must be stated that Democritus taught nothing new, but simply what he had learnt from the Egyptians, directly or indirectly.

His doctrine on the universal distribution of fire atoms is based upon a magical principle: if the atom is an ingredient of the world, then it would be universally distributed.

Furthermore, Democritus enters history as a magician, and since there is historical evidence that he visited the Egyptian priests, it is evident that magic was part of the training which he must have received from them.

(Antisthenes: Treatise on Succession; Herodotus; Origen; Diogenes Laertius: Bk. 9 p. 443; Zeller's Hist. of Phil. p. 77).

3. *His Books are doubtful in authorship.*

Several important facts must be noted in connection with the books which are said to have been written by Democritus:-

(a) A large number of books which appears in a list in the 9th Book of Diogenes, Laertius, does not appear elsewhere in the usual textbooks on the history of Greek Philosophy; while Zeller asserts that the genuineness of these books cannot be determined upon the evidence of the fragments. (Zeller's Hist. of Phil. p. 77). It seems that his list of publications remains doubtful in authorship.

(b) More than 60 different subjects are treated and they include Ethics, Physics, Astronomy, Botany, Zoology, Poetry, Medicine, Dialectics, Military Science, and Law; also books on Magic, including divination.

(c) We are informed by Diogenes Laertius that this large list of books was compiled by Thrasyllus (about 20 A. D.) who was a student of the school of Plato, and also a member of Aristotle's movement, which had for its purpose, the compilation of Greek philosophy. (Zeller's Hist. of Phil. p. 13-14) (Diogenes Laertius Bk. 9 p. 455-461).

VI. *The Four Qualities and Four Elements.*

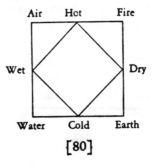

The history of the following ancient theory of *"The Four Qualities and Four Elements"*, provides the world with the evidence of the Egyptian origin of the doctrines of (a) Opposites or Contraries, (b) Change or Transmutation and (c) the life and function of the universe is due to either of four elements: fire, or water, or earth or air.

1. This ancient theory was expressed by a diagram formed by outer and inner squares.

2. The corners of the outer square carried the names of the elements: fire, water, earth and air.

3. The corners of the inner square, being at the mid points of the sides of the outer square, carried the four fundamental qualities, the hot, the dry, the cold and the wet.

4. The diagram explains that fire is hot and dry; earth is dry and cold; water is cold and wet; and air is wet and hot.

5. Accordingly water is an embodiment of cold and wet qualities, and when the cold quality is replaced by the hot quality, the element water is changed into the element air, with the wet and hot qualities.

6. Consequently, transmutation is definitely implied in the teaching of this symbol.

7. It is the oldest teaching of physical science and has been traced to the Egyptians, as far back as 5000 B. C.

8. It shows that Plato and Aristotle (who had been credited with the authorship of this teaching) derived their doctrines or portions of them from the Egyptians. (Rosicrucian Digest, May 1952, p. 175).

CHAPTER VI:

The Athenian Philosophers.

1. Socrates: (i) IIis Life (ii) Doctrines (iii) Summary of Conclusions.

(i) LIFE OF SOCRATES

(a) *Date and place of birth.*

Socrates was born in Athens, in the year 469 B. C. He was the son of Sophroniscus, a sculptor, and Phaenarete, a midwife. Very little is known about his early years; but we are told that he was brought up in the profession of his father, and that he called himself not only a pupil of Prodicus and Aspasia, (which statement suggests that he might have learnt from them, music, geometry and gymnastics): but also a self taught philosopher, according to Xenophon in the Symposium. Up to the age of 40, his life appears to be a complete blank: the first mention being made of him, when he served as an ordinary soldier in the sieges of Potidaea and Delium between (432-429) B. C. (Trial and Death of Socrates: F. J. Church: p. 15 of Introduction).

(b) *His economic status and personality.*

Socrates did not accept fees for what he taught, and he became so poor, that his wife Xanthippe became very dissatisfied with domestic conditions.

He believed that he possessed (*Daimonion τi*) a divine something, i.e., a divine voice which advised and guided him in the great crises of his life. (Turner's Hist. of Phil. p. 78-79; and Plato's Apology).

(c) *His Condemnation and death in 399 B. C.*

After the accustomed speeches of the accusers: (Miletus, Anytus and Lycon); Socrates followed with his defense, at

[83]

the conclusion of which, the judges voted 281 to 220, **and** Socrates was condemned to death.

As a parting word, he addressed himself both to those **who** voted against him, and those who voted in his favour. In **the** case of the former, he rebuked them by predicting that **evil** would befall them, in consequence of their crime in condemn-ing him.

In the case of the latter, he not only consoled them **with** the assurance that no evil could come to a good man **either** in life or in death; but also expressed to them his idea **about** immortality. "Death is either an eternal and dreamless sleep, wherein there is no sensation at all; or it is a journey **to** another, and a better world, where are the famous men of old". Whichever alternative be true, death is not an evil, **but** a good. His death is willed by the gods, and he is content. (Plato's Apology Chapters 25-28).

His death was delayed through a state religious ceremonial, and he remained in prison for 30 days. We are told that dur-ing this time, he was visited by his friends, who consisted of the inner circle, and also his wife Xanthippe; that this **was** the occasion of his discourse concerning the immortality of **the** soul; that he could have escaped from death if he wished; because his friends visited him before day-break and offered to set him free; but that he refused the offer. Accordingly Socrates drank the hemlock and died. (Plato Phaedo;) (Xeno-phon Memorabilia IV, 8, 2).

(d) Crito's account:

Crito, on the night before the death of Socrates, while he was in prison, on behalf of the company of visitors, made a final appeal to him to permit them to secure his escape, and spoke as follows:-

"O, my Socrates, I beseech you for the last time to listen to me and save yourself. For to me your death will be more than a single disaster: not only shall I lose a friend the like of whom I shall never find again, but many persons, who do not know you and me well, will think that I might have saved you, if I had been willing to spend money, but that I neglected to do so. And what character could be more disgraceful than the character of caring more for money than for one's friends? The world will never believe that we were anxious to save you, but that you yourself refused to escape.

"Tell me this Socrates. Surely you are not anxious about me and your other friends, and afraid, lest, if you escape, the informers should say that we stole you away, and get us into trouble, and involve us in a great deal of expense, or perhaps in the loss of all our property, and it may be, bring some other punishment upon us besides? If you have any fear of that kind, dismiss it.

"For of course we are bound to run those risks, and still greater risks than those if necessary, in saving you. So do not, I beseech you, refuse to listen to me."

Then Socrates replied: "I am anxious about that, Crito, and about much besides," and Crito continued the appeal:-

"Then have no fear on that score. There are men who, for no very large sum, are ready to bring you out of prison into safety, and then, you know, these informers are cheaply bought, and there will be no need to spend much on them.

"My fortune is at your disposal, and I think that it is sufficient, and if you have any feeling about making use of my money, there are strangers in Athens, whom you know, ready to use theirs, and one of them, Simmias of Thebes, who actually brought enough for the purpose. And Cebes and many others, are ready too.

"And therefore, I repeat, do not shrink from saving yourself, on that ground. And do not let what you said in court (that if you went into exile, you would not know what to do with yourself), stand in your way: for there are many places for you to go to, where you will be welcomed.

"If you choose to go to Thessaly, I have friends there who will make much of you, and shelter you from any annoyance from the people of Thessaly.

"Consider then, Socrates; or rather the time for consideration is past; we must resolve, and there is only one plan possible. Everything must be done tonight. If we delay any longer, we are lost.

"O, Socrates, I implore you not to refuse to listen to me." (Plato's Crito C. 3-5).

(e) *Phaedo's account of the final scene just before the death of Socrates.*

In answer to another question from Echecrates, Phaedo replied: I will try to tell you the whole story:-

"On the previous days, I and the others had always met in the morning at the court, where the trial was held, which was close to the prison; and then we would go in to Socrates.

"We used to wait each morning until the prison was opened, conversing; for it was not opened early. When it was opened we used to go in to Socrates, and we generally spent the whole day with him. But on that morning we met earlier than usual, for the evening before we had learnt, on leaving the prison, that the ship had arrived from Delos. So we arranged to be at the usual place as early as possible. When we reached the prison, the porter, who generally let us in came out to us and bade us wait a little, and not to go in until he himself summoned us; for the 'Eleven' were releasing Socrates from his fetters and giving him directions for his death.

"In no great while he returned and bade us enter. So we went in and found Socrates just released. When Xanthippe saw us, she wailed aloud, and cried in her woman's way: 'This is the last time: Socrates, that you will talk with your friends, or they with you.' And Socrates glanced at Crito and said, 'Crito, let her be taken home'. So some of Crito's servants led her away; weeping bitterly and beating her breasts. And it was about sunset, and the servant of the Eleven after bidding Socrates farewell, gave him the instructions as to how to take the poison, and then handed it to him. Socrates took the cup, and drank the poison cheerfully, and then walked about until his legs felt heavy. And when he had lain down, he made his last request to Crito in the following words: I owe a cock to Asclepius, do not forget to pay it. By this time the poison took effect and he passed away." (Plato Phaedo C. 3 and 65).

(ii) THE DOCTRINES OF SOCRATES

i. *The doctrine of Nous*, i.e., mind or an Intelligent Cause, in order to account for God and Creation. He is credited with the teleological premise: whatever exists for a useful purpose is the work of an Intelligence. (Xenophon Memorabilia I, 4, 2; Wm. Turner's Hist. of Phil. p. 82).

ii. *The doctrine of the Supreme Good:-*

The Supreme good i.e., the summum bonum is equated both with happiness and with knowledge. This however is not merely *eutuchia* which depends upon external conditions and accidents of fortune; but is (*eupraxia*), a well-being, which is conditioned by good action. This is an attainment in which man becomes godlike through self denial of external needs and the cultivation of the mind: for happiness comes not through the perishable things of the external world, but through the things that endure, which are within us. (Xenophon Memorabilia I, 5, 4.) Wm. Turner's Hist. of Phil. p. 83).

iii. *The doctrines of opposites and harmony*:

(a) *Odd and even are the elements of numbers.* One is definite but the other is unlimited, and the unit is the product both of odd and even. Hence the universe consists of opposites: the finite and the infinite, the male and the female; the odd and the even; the left and right.

(b) *Harmony is the union of opposites.*

(Plato's Phaedo C. 15; Wm. Turner's Hist. of Phil. p. 41; 47).

(Zeller's Hist. of Phil. p. 61).

iv. *The Doctrines Concerning the Soul*:

(a) The immortality of the Soul
(b) The transmigration of the Soul

(c) The Salvation of the Soul:-

The purpose of philosophy is the salvation of the Soul, whereby it feeds upon the truth congenial to its divine nature, and thus escapes from the wheel of re-birth, and finally attains the consummation of unity with God. (Zeller's Hist. of Phil. p. 50-56; Roger's Hist. of Phil. p. 29 and 60; Wm. Turner's Hist. of Phil. p. 41 and 48).

(d) The body is the tomb of the Soul

(e) The aspirations of the Soul:-

There is a realm of true reality, which is above the world of sense. To this the Soul aspires.

v. *The doctrine of Self-knowledge: Know thyself (seauton gnothi)*.

Self-knowledge is the basis of true knowledge. The Mysteries required as a first step, the mastery of the passions, which made room for the occupation of unlimited powers. Hence, as a second step, the Neophyte was required to search within himself for the new powers which had taken possession of him. The Egyptians consequently wrote on their temples: "Man, know thyself". (Zeller's Hist. of Phil. p. 105; S. Clymer's Fire Philosophy p. 203).

vi. *Astrology and Geology:*

There was a suspicion that Socrates was also engaged in the study of Astrology and Geology, and that he taught these subjects, for in his defense before the Athenian judges, he stated that the more formidable of his accusers tried to persuade them with lies, that one Socrates, a wise man, was speculating about the heavens and about things beneath the earth, and that he was capable of making the worse appear the better reason. (Plato's Apology C. 2).

This suspicion is further supported by the indictment brought against Socrates, and which reads as follows:- "Miletus, the son of Miletus, of the deme Pitthis, on his oath,

brings the following accusation against Socrates, the son of
Sophroniscus, of the deme Alopece.

"Socrates commits a crime by not believing in the gods of
the city, and by introducing new divinities. He also commits a
crime by corrupting the youth. Penalty, death."

(Plato's Apology C. 24; C. 18 and 19).

There is still a third source from which the suspicion arose
that Socrates was engaged also in Astrology and Geology.
This was the caricature of Socrates, published by Aristophanes
in his comedy: the Clouds, as follows:-

"Socrates is a miserable recluse, who speaks a great deal of
absurd and amusing nonsense about Physics, and declares that
Zeus is dethroned, that Rotation reigns in his stead, and that
the new divinities are Air, which holds the earth suspended,
Ether, the Clouds and Tongue.

"He professes to possess the power of Belial, which enables
him to make the worse appear the better reason, and his
teachings cause children to beat their parents."

(Aristophanes Clouds, 828 and 380; Life and Trial of
Socrates; F. J. Church: Introduction p. 18).

(iii) *Summary of Conclusions.*

1. *Life and Personality of Socrates.*

There are two circumstances in the life of Socrates which
demand our attention: (a) he is said to have been completely
unknown up to the age of 40 and (b) to have lived a life of
poverty. These circumstances point to secrecy in training, and
poverty as conditions of his life; and as such, they coincide
with the requirements of the Mystery System of Egypt, and
her secret schools, whether in the land of Egypt or abroad,
which exacted the vows of secrecy and poverty from all Neophytes and Initiates. All aspirants of the Mysteries had to
receive secret training and preparation, and Socrates was no
exception. He alone of the three Athenian philosophers deserves the appellation of a true Master Mason. Plato was a

great coward and Aristotle was greater still. At the execution
of Socrates, Plato fled to Megara to the lodge of Euclid, and
Aristotle when indicted fled in exile to Calchis.

(Clement of Alexandria: Stromata Bk. 5. C. 7 and 9; Plutarch on "Isis and Osiris" Sec. 9-11; Plato's Apology C. 8; 17;
Phaedo C. 10; 13; 32; 63).

2. *The Doctrines*:-

(i) *The doctrine of the Nous or an Intelligent Cause.*

With reference to this doctrine, we find that it is also credited to Anaxagoras, who is said to have lived between 500 and
430 B. C. and who therefore antedated Socrates (469-399
B. C.) in expounding it (Wm. Turner's Hist. of Phil. p. 63;
p. 82).

Secondly, further examination shows that the doctrine of
the Nous is also a direct inference from the doctrine of Cognition, as credited to Democritus (460-360 B. C.), who is
credited with stating that fire atoms are distributed through
the universe, and that mind is composed of fire atoms.

Therefore it can be inferred (a) that mind fills or is distributed through the universe and (b) since only like can
produce like, then the mind of the Universe must have been
produced by a mind which is its source.

(Wm. Turner's Hist. of Phil. p. 68; Zeller's Hist. of Phil.
p. 80).

Thirdly, this doctrine of the Nous, is a doctrine that originated from the Ancient Mysteries of Egypt, where the God
Osiris was represented in all Egyptian temples by the symbol
of an Open Eye. This symbol indicated not only sight that
transcends time and space, but also the omniscience of God,
as the Great Mind which created and which directs the Universe. This symbol is carried as a decoration in all modern
Masonic lodges and has the same meaning. (Ancient Mysteries: C. H. Vail p. 189).

(ii) *The doctrine of the Supreme Good*:-

This doctrine of the Supreme Good or Summum Bonum is likewise a very ancient doctrine which takes us back to the Egyptian Mysteries.

As stated in the books on Greek philosophy and by Socrates, it is only in part, and consequently a mistaken notion of the original doctrine has resulted. To say that the supreme good is happiness, that happiness is well-being, that well-being is knowledge, and that knowledge is virtue, is the same thing as saying that the Supreme Good is virtue.

(Xenophon Memorabilia I 4, 5; Wm. Turner's Hist. of Phil. p. 81-83).

In the Egyptian Mysteries, however, the concept of the Supreme Good is expressed as the purpose of virtue, and that is the salvation of the Soul, by liberating it from the ten bodily fetters. This process of liberation is a process of purification both of mind and of body: the former by the study of philosophy and science, and the latter by bodily ascetic disciplines. This training was continued from the baptism of water, and was subsequently followed by the baptism of fire, when the candidate had made the necessary progress. This process transformed man and made him godlike, and fitted him for union with God.

The concept of the Supreme Good, which originally came from the Egyptian Mysteries is the earliest theory of salvation: and Socrates must have derived this doctrine from that source, or indirectly from the Pythagoreans.

(Plato's Phaedo C. 31; 33-34; Ancient Mysteries, C. H. Vail p. 24-25; Fire Philosophy, R. S. Clymer p. 19; 74; 80).

(iii) *The following doctrines are generally admitted as having been derived from the Pythagoreans*:

(a) Transmigration of the Soul
(b) The immortality of the Soul
(c) The tomb of the Soul is the body.

[91]

(d) The doctrines of opposites and harmony.

Since doctrines (a), (b), (c) and (d) originated from the Pythagoreans, and since the Pythagoreans derived them from the Egyptians, then their Egyptian origin, direcly or indirectly becomes evident.

(Roger's Hist. of Phil. p. 29 and 60; Turner's Hist. of Phil. p. 41 and 48; Plato's Phaedo).

(iv) *Astrology and Geology*:

From (a) the indictment (b) his defense before the Athenian Judges and (c) the caricature by Aristophanes in the Clouds, we discover that Socrates was suspected of being a student of Nature, and of introducing new divinities into Athens.

Again it must be stated, that under the Mystery System of Egypt, the study of Nature was a requirement, and since the Athenians prosecuted and condemned Socrates to death, for engaging in this study and spreading the knowledge, they must have regarded the new ideas as foreign or of Egyptian origin.

(Plato's Apology C. 24-28; Ancient Mysteries, C. H. Vail p. 24-25).

(v) *The Doctrine of Self-knowledge*:

The doctrine of self-knowledge, for centuries attributed to Socrates is now definitely known to have originated from the Egyptian Temples, on the outside of which the words "Man, know thyself" were written.

It is evident that Socrates taught nothing new, because his doctrines are eclectic containing elements from Anaxagoras, Democritus, Heraclitus, Parmenides and Pythagoras, and finally have been traced to the teachings of the Egyptian Mystery System.

(Fire Philosophy, S. R. Clymer p. 203).

vi) *The importance of the farewell conversations of Socrates with his pupils and friends at the prison*:

In examining what took place during the farewell conversations of Socrates with his pupils and friends, at least five points should be noted:-
(a) The subject of the Conversations
(b) The determination of his friends to smuggle him away
(c) His refusal to accept liberation
(d) His dying request, which was addressed to Crito, whom he asked to pay an important debt for him
(e) The value of those conversations, in their present form in literature.

Now the question arises, what is the meaning and significance of these five points? The answers and conclusions are as follows:-

(a) As the subject of the conversations dealt with the immortality and salvation of the Soul, we at once recognize the fact that this was the central theme of the Ancient Mysteries, and consequently that Socrates was acquainted with the doctrines.

Moreover, when we read the Phaedo and the doctrines, both of Opposites and Recollection which he had advanced in proof of immortality, we are convinced that he must have received his training from the Mystery System of Egypt, in connection with which there were Hierophants and qualified teachers.

(b) Secondly, in dealing with the behavior of his friends, in their determination to smuggle him away, we are dealing with their attempt to render help to a brother in distress.

This was the life that Initiates were expected to live, for brotherhood was another great principle upon which, the Egyptian Mysteries laid emphasis. Evidently, Socrates was a "Brother Initiate" of the Egyptian Mysteries, since it comprised one universal brotherhood.

(c) Thirdly, in dealing with the refusal of Socrates to accept liberation, again we are dealing with a type of behaviour, which singles him out as an advanced Initiate of the Ancient Mysteries of Egypt. In the paths to mastery and victory, the

Mystery System regarded unselfishness or sacrifice as an advanced stage of attainment, which must be accomplished before unlimited power could be bestowed upon the candidate. It is true that Anaxagoras escaped for his life and in like manner Plato and Aristotle; but this only serves to show that Socrates had reached a higher degree in the Mysteries than all of them. This necessitated training and the training centre was Egypt.

(d) Fourthly, with reference to the dying request of Socrates, addressed to Crito, in which he asked him to pay a certain debt, we again encounter another of the great ideals essential to the life of an Initiate. This in the teaching of the Mysteries embraces the exercise of a cardinal virtue i.e., justice; a practice which the Candidate must adopt, in order that his sense of value might also develop.

Here again the action of Socrates reveals that he was a Brother Initiate, with a high sense of justice and honesty, since he did not wish to die without discharging all his obligations. Certainly, the dying request of Socrates reveals him as a loyal member of the Mystery System of Egypt.

(e) Fifthly and finally, what value may we attach to the literature which deals with the farewell conversations of Socrates with his friends and pupils? Since this literature embraces a man whose beliefs and practices coincide with those of the Initiates of the Ancient Mysteries of Egypt, then we may regard the study of Xenophon's Memorabilia, Plato's Apology, the Phaedo, Euthyphro, Crito and Timaeus as valuable specimens of literature of the Mysteries, or Masonic World.

Ancient Mysteries; C. H. Vail C. 24-25; also C. 32).
(The Phaedo of Plato; The Timaeus of Plato).
(R. S. Clymer; Fire Philosophy C. 44; 49; 67; 75).

2. Plato: (i) Early Life (ii) Travels (iii) Disputed Writings (iv) His Doctrines (v) Summary of Conclusions.

(i) *His Early Life:*
Plato is said to have been born at Athens in 427 B. C., and

that his father's name was Aristo, and his mother's name was Perictione, who was a relative of Solon.

Little information is known about his early life and training: but there is a supposition that because his parents were wealthy, he must have had such educational opportunities as were available to a wealthy youth. He is said to have studied the doctrines of Heraclitus under Cratylus, and to have been a pupil of Socrates for eight years. It is also said that he was a soldier. (Roger's Student Hist. of Philosophy p. 76) (Wm. Turner's Hist. of Philosophy p. 93) (Will. Durant's Story of Phil.)

(ii) (a) *His Travels*:

He was 28 years old, when Socrates died (i.e., 399 B. C.), and together with the other pupils of Socrates, he fled from Athens to Euclid at Megara for Safety. He kept away from Athens for 12 years, during which time, it is also said that apart from visiting Euclid, he travelled (a) to Southern Italy where he met the remnant of Pythagoreans, (b) to Syracuse in Sicily, where, through Dion, he met Dionysius to whom he became a Tutor: who subsequently caused him to be sold as a slave, and (c) to Egypt.

(Fuller's Hist. of Philosophy) (Roger's Student's Hist. of Philosophy) (Wm. Turner's Hist. of Phil. p. 94) (Diogenes Laertius Bk. III, p. 277).

(ii) (b) *His Academy*

Plato is said to have returned to Athens in 387 B. C. when a middle aged man of 40 years and to have opened an Academy in a gymnasium on the western suburbs of Athens over which he presided for 20 years. He is said to have taught the following subjects (a) Political Science (b) Statesmanship (c) Mathematics (d) Dialectics, and it is said that the curriculum was based upon the educational principles advocated in the Republic.

(Fuller's Hist. of Philosophy: Plato's Life) (B. D. Alexander's Hist. of Philosophy p. 68) (Roger's Students Hist. of

Philosophy p. 72) (Wm. Turner's Hist. of Philosophy p. 122-123).

(iii) *His Writings are disputed and doubted by modern scholarship.*

There are 36 *dialogues and a number of letters, which Plato is supposed to have written: but which are disputed and doubted by modern scholarship.*

(a) Grote states that Plato has written only those dialogues that bear his name.

(b) Schaarsmidt states that only nine of the 36 dialogues are genuine while

(c) Aristotle considered the Platonic dialogues as nine in number, namely The Laws, Timaeus, Phaedo, Symposium, Phaedrus, Georgias, Theaetus, Philebus and the Republic, which he thought are genuine.

(d) Of the remaining 27 dialogues some scholars contend that the youthful dialogues should be included with the genuine ones, and these are the Apology, Crito, Enthydemus, Laches, Lysis and Protagoras, and

(e) Of the remaining 21 dialogues scholars suggest that those which were not written by Plato must have been written by his pupils (B. D. Alexander's Hist. of Phil. p. 68).

(iv) THE DOCTRINES OF PLATO:

The doctrines attributed to Plato are scattered over a wide area of literature: being found in piecemeal throughout what are called dialogues; but particularly in connection with—

(I) the theory of ideas and its application to natural phenomena which includes the doctrines of (a) the real and unreal (b) the Nous (mind) and (c) Creation.

(II) the ethical doctrines concerning (A) the highest good (B) definition of virtue and (C) the cardinal virtues.

(III) the doctrine of the Ideal State whose attributes are compared with the attributes of the soul and justice. Following this order, they are as follows:

(I) *The Theory of Ideas*

A. *Definition of Ideas*. This may be expressed in the following syllogism:

The idea (retaining its unity, unchangeableness and perfection) is the element of reality in a thing.

The idea is the concept by which a thing is known. Therefore the concept by which a thing is known is the element of reality in a thing (*To on*).

It follows also, that since the concept or idea of a thing is real, then the concrete thing itself is unreal.

(Timaeus 51) (Phaedrus 247).

B. *The application of the theory of Ideas to natural Phenomena.*

In view of the definition of the Idea, three doctrines have resulted:-

(a) *The doctrine of the real and unreal.*

The things which we see around us are the phenomena of nature, they belong to the earthly realm, they are only copies (*Eidola*) of their prototypes (*paradeigmata*), the Ideas and noumena, which dwell in the heavenly realm. The Ideas are real and perfect, but the phenomena are unreal and imperfect; and it is the function of philosophy to enable the mind to rise above the contemplation of the visible copies of Ideas, and advance to a knowledge of the Ideas themselves. (The Phaedrus 250).

There is however, something common between them, because the phenomena partake of the Idea (*metechei*). This participation is an imitation (*mimesis*), but it is so imperfect that natural phenomena fall far short of Ideas.

(Parmenides 132 D) (Aristotle's Metaphysics I, 6; 987b, 9).

[97]

(b) *The doctrine of the Nous or World Soul.*

This teaches that the universe are living animals and that they are endowed with the most perfect and intelligent souls; that if God had made the world as perfect as the nature of matter allowed, that He must have endowed it with a perfect soul. This soul acts as mediator between the Ideas and natural phenomena, and is the cause of life, motion, order, and knowledge in the universe. (Timaeus, 30, 35).

(c) *The doctrine of a Demiurgos in Creation (Cosmology)*

In the myth of creation found in the Timaeus, we find the doctrine on Creation, as it is ascribed to Plato's authorship, as follows:-

Out of chaos, which was ruled by necessity, God the Demiurgos or Creator, made order, by fashioning the phenomena of matter according to the eternal prototypes (i.e., the Ideas) in as perfect a manner, as the imperfection of matter would allow. He next created the Gods, and ordered them to fashion the body of man, while He himself, made the soul of man, from the same material as that of the world soul.

The soul of man is a self-moving principle and is responsible for life, motion and consciousness in the body.

(Myth of creation in Timaeus; Wm. Turner's Hist. of Philosophy, p. 109-110).

(II *The Ethical Doctrines*

The ethical doctrines that have been attributed to Plato are (A) that of the highest good, i.e., the Summum Bonum (B) the connotation of virtue and (C) the reduction of the virtues to four and the place of wisdom among them (A) as something subjective, and as an earthly experience, the highest good is happiness: but as an objective attainment, it is the Idea of good, and consequently identified with God.

Therefore the purpose of man's life is freedom from the fetters of the body, in which the soul is confined, and the practice of virtue and wisdom, makes him like a God, even while on earth.

(B) and (C)

Virtue is the order, the health and the harmony of the soul.

There are many virtues, but the greatest is wisdom. All virtues may be reduced to the four cardinal virtues: wisdom, fortitude, temperance and justice.

(Symposium 204E); (Theaetetus 176A); (Phaedo 64 sqq.) (The Republic IV, 441, 443).

(III) *The Ideal State (The Republic)*

The doctrine attributed to Plato in the field of civics is the doctrine of the Ideal state whose attributes are compared with the attributes of the soul and justice.

In a state, virtue should be the chief aim, and unless philosophers become rulers, or rulers become thorough students of philosophy, there will be unceasing troubles for states and humanity at large. The Ideal state is modelled upon the individual soul, and just as the soul has three parts, so also should the state have three parts: the rulers, the warriors, and the workers.

(Republic VI, 490 sqq.; V, 478; III, 415).

Similarly, just as the harmony of the soul depends upon the proper subordination of its parts, so also does the state depend upon the proper subordination of its parts, in order to enjoy peace.

Here Plato introduces the allegory of the charioteer and the winged steeds, in order to show that virtue is to the soul as justice is to the state:- One horse is of noble origin: while the other is ignoble; and consequently they cannot agree. As the noble horse strives to mount up to the heavenly regions which are suitable to its nature: so the other tries to drag him down. Likewise in dealing with the soul, it is the proper subordination of its parts, that enables the noble in man to attain its excellence; so also in dealing with the state, it is justice, or the proper subordination of the different classes, that makes it an Ideal State.

(Roger's Students Hist. of Phil. p. 83); (Plato's Republic).

(v) SUMMARY OF CONCLUSIONS.

The doctrines of Plato are eclectic and point to Egyptian origin.

1. The doctrine of the real and unreal to represent doctrine found in the comparison between natural phenomena and the Ideas, is only an instance of the application of the doctrine of opposites. Here the things of this world have their corresponding types in the heavenly realm; here the Ideas correspond to Being, while the natural phenomena correspond to not-Being. But the doctrine of opposites may be traced back not only to Socrates, Democritus, Parmenides and the Pythagoreans, but further back to its original source, i.e., the Egyptian Mystery System, where the principle of opposites was represented not only by pairs of male and female Gods, such as Osiris and Isis, but also by pairs of pillars in the front of all the Egyptian temples.

(Memphite Theology in Kingship and the Gods, by Frankfort, C. 3, p. 25-26 and 35).

(Herodotus I, 6-26) (Ancient Egypt by John Kendrick, Bk. I, p. 339).

(Egyptian Religion by Frankfort, p. 64, 73, 88).

(Zeller's Hist. of Phil. p. 61).

(The Phaedo C. 15, 16, 49).

II. *The doctrine of the Nous or World Soul is a principle of Egyptian magic:*

Plato is credited with expressing this doctrine in the form of a simile, in which he compares the world to a living animal, which is composed of Souls. One being made perfect and responsible for the life, motion and knowledge of the animal or universe.

This doctrine may be traced not only to (a) Democritus who based his teaching about the fire atoms of the soul, and cognition upon the magical principle of the Egyptians: "that the qualities of an animal are distributed throughout its parts."

(Golden Bough by Frazer) (Hist. of Phil., B. D. Alexander, p. 40).

(Wm. Turner, Hist. of Phil., p. 68), but also to (b) Anaxagoras, who is said to have advanced the Nous (mind) as responsible for creating order out of chaos, and which is omnipotent and omniscient.

(History of Philosophy, Wm. Turner, p. 63).

The doctrine of the *Nous* as a matter of fact, originated from (c) the Mystery System of Egypt, in connection with which, the God Osiris was represented in all Egyptian temples, by the symbol of an Open Eye, referred to elsewhere.

This symbol indicated not only sight that transcended space and time: but also omniscience, as the Great Mind which created and which still directs the universe. This symbol also forms a part of the decoration of all Masonic lodges of the modern world and dates back to the Osirian or Sun worship of the Egyptians more than 5000 B. C. This same notion was also represented by the Egyptians by a God with eyes all over Him and was known as the "All seeing Eye."

(Zeller's Hist. of Phil., p. 809).
(The Ancient Mysteries, C. H. Vail, p. 189)
(Max Muller: Egyptian Mythology).

III. *The doctrine of the Demiurge in Creation.*

This doctrine which is ascribed to the authorship of Plato, did not by any means originate from Plato. It was not only a current doctrine at the time of Plato, but was well known among the Eastern Ancient nations and taught by them many centuries before his time (427-347 B. C.).

History tells us that the Persians taught this doctrine more than six centuries B. C. through their leader Zoroaster. History also tells us that Pythagoras (500 B. C.), taught the same doctrine expressed in terms of Monads. The universe consisted of two unities, i.e., (a) the Unity from which the series of numbers or beings is derived, being absolute Unity, which is the source of all, i.e., the Monad of Monads or the God of Gods and (b) the One, i.e., the first in the series of derived numbers or beings. It is opposed to and limited by plurality, and therefore it is relative unity, i.e., a created Monad or God (a *Demiurge*), consequently the opposition between the One and the many is the source of all the rest. Furthermore, history likewise tells us that the original source of the doctrine of a Demiurge in creation was Egypt, and it dates back to the creation story of Egypt 4000 B. C. which is to be found in the account given by the Memphite Theology: an inscription on a stone, now kept in the British Museum. It contains the theological and cosmological views of the Egyptians which date back to the very beginning of Egyptian history, when the first dynasties had made their new capital at Memphis, the city of the God Ptah, i.e., about 4000 B. C., or even earlier.

The Egyptian cosmology must be presented in three parts; each part being supplementary to the other, and presenting a complete philosophy by their combination. Part (I) deals with the Gods of chaos, part (II) deals with the Gods of order and arrangement in creation, and part (III) deals with the Primate of the Gods, through whose *Logos* creation was accomplished. In part (I) pre-creation or chaos is represented by (i) Ptah, the Primate of the Gods, emerging from the primeval waters Nun in the form of a Hill, Ta-tjenen, i.e., The Risen Land (ii) Atum, i.e., Atom, the sun God, immediately joining Ptah, by emerging also from the chaotic waters Nun, and sitting upon him (the Hill).

(iii) A description of the other qualities within the chaos follows:- There are four pairs of male and female Gods in the form of frogs and serpents. Their names are (a) Nun and Naunet, the primeval ocean and primeval matter; (b) Huh and Hauhet, the Illimitable and the Boundless, (c) Kuk and Kauket, Darkness and Obscurity; and (d) Amon and Amaunet, the Hidden and concealed ones. (Memphite Theology in Ancient Egyptian Religion by Frankfort, p. 10, p. 21; Frankfort's Intellectual Adventure of Man, p. 10, 21, 52).

In part (II) the Gods of order and arrangement are represented as follows:-

The same first pair of pre-creation Gods are together present, i.e., Ptah, the primeval Hill, who is the thought and word of all the Gods, together with Atum, who rests upon Ptah.

Atum, i.e., Atom, having absorbed the thought and creative power of Ptah, then proceeds with the work of Creation. He names four pairs of parts of his own body, which become Gods, and in this way, eight Gods are created, who together with himself become nine Gods in one family or Godhead, called the Ennead.

N. B.

Magic is the key to the interpretaton of ancient religions and philosophy.

(a) Part (III) tells of the specific powers of Ptah, which Atum absorbs, but does not tell us how He absorbs them.

(b) Part (I) tells us how, for it describes the movement of Atum, as emerging from the primeval waters, and sitting upon Ptah (the risen land or hill). It however does not give us the reason for Atum's movement: a behavior which can be understood, only when we apply to its interpretation, the key of magical principles.

(c) *The Magical Principle*

Now, what is the magical principle involved in Atum's behavior? It is this:-

"The qualities or attributes of entities, human or divine, are distributed throughout their various parts, and contact with such entities, releases those qualities."

(d) It is now clear that by making contact with Ptah, Atum immediately received the attributes of Ptah's creative thought and speech and omnipotence and became the instrument and the Logos and the Demiurge, through whom the task of creation was undertaken and completed.

(Dr. Frazer's Golden Bough).

(e) It is also clear that according to the Memphite Theology, the doctrines of a Demiurge and created Gods originated from the Egyptian religion and Mystery System, and not from Plato who lived from 427 to 347 B. C.

(Ancient Egyptian Religion: Memphite Theology by Frankfort, p. 20 and 23).

(Intellectual Adventure of Ancient Man, by Frankfort, p. 21, and 51-60).

(The Egyptian Book of the Dead, c. 17).

(The Golden Bough, by Dr. Frazer—on Magic).

(The Mediterranean World, by Sandford, p. 182).

(History of Philosophy, by Weber, p. 21-22).

(The Cure of the woman who touched the hem of Christ's garment: Mark, chapter 5, verses 25-34).

(The cure of several people who held the kerchiefs of St. Paul: Acts, chapter 19, verse 12).

N.B.

The Memphite Theology will be dealt with in a separate chapter to show the origin of Greek Philosophy.

IV. *The doctrines of (A) the highest good (B) virtue and (C) the cardinal virtues.*

N.B.

This is really the earliest theory of salvation and it originated from the Egyptian Mysteries but not from Plato.

(A) The main purpose of the Egyptian Mysteries was the salvation of the human soul. The Egyptians believed the human body to be a prison house, where the soul is chained by ten fetters. This condition not only kept man separated from God, but made him subject to the wheel of re-birth or re-incarnation.

In order to escape from the effects of his condition, two requirements had to be fulfilled by the Neophyte:-

(i) He must keep the Ten Commandments taught by the Mysteries, for by such a discipline, he would gain conquest over the fetters of the soul, and liberate it, so as to make its development possible, and

(ii) he now being well qualified and duly prepared, must undergo a series of initiations, in order to develop his soul from the human stage to that of a God. Such a transformation was known as salvation. It placed the Neophyte in harmony with nature, man and God. It deified him, i.e., made him become godlike; and this attainment was known as the highest good.

According to this theory of salvation, man is expected to work out his own salvation, without a mediator between himself and his God.

(B) Plato defines virtue as the order or discipline of the soul. This meaning we accept, since it agrees with the purpose of the ten commandments of the Mysteries.

The doctrines of the ten virtues and the ten fetters are as old as the Egyptian history itself. Each commandment or discipline represented a principle of virtue, and the function of each virtue was to remove a fetter. Hence a life of virtue was antecedent and preparatory to those further experiences, i.e., the initiations which led to gradual perfection and the divinity of the Neophyte.

(C) Plato is also credited with having reduced all virtues to four cardinal virtues, and with assigning the highest place among them to wisdom, as follows:- wisdom, fortitude, temperance and justice.

We are also informed through the history of philosophy, that Socrates, the alleged teacher of Plato, taught that wisdom was the equivalent of all virtue. This divergence of opinion between pupil and teacher is significant, since it points to the fact that both of them simply speculated about a system of Ethics which was current in the ancient world, and which neither of them had produced.

This system of Ethics as has already been mentioned belonged to the Mystery System of Egypt, which required Neophytes in preparation for initiation, to keep the following ten commandments, underlying which were ten principles of virtue:-

The Neophyte must (I) control his thoughts (II) control his actions (III) have devotion of purpose (IV) have faith in the ability of his master to teach him the truth (V) have faith in himself to assimilate the truth (VI) have faith in himself to wield the truth (VII) be free from resentment under the experience of persecution (VIII) be free from resentment under experience of wrong, (IX) cultivate the ability to distinguish between right and wrong and (X) cultivate the ability to distinguish between the real and the unreal (he must have a sense of values).

If we now compare the order in the above outline with the order in which the cardinal virtues are said to be arranged, we shall immediately see that the first place which wisdom occupies among the virtues was given to it by the Egyptian Mysteries, and not by Plato. Consequently in (I) and (II) from the control of thoughts and actions, we derive the virtue of wisdom; in (VI) from freedom of resentment under persecution, we derive the virtue of fortitude; in (IX) and (X) from an ability to distinguish between right and wrong, and between the real and unreal, we derive the virtues of justice and temperance.

(Plato's Republic, c. IV, 44, and 443).
(Ancient Mysteries by C. H. Vail, p. 25 also 109-112).
(Wm. Turner's History of Philosophy, p. 115).
(Zeller's History of Philosophy, p. 155-157).

V. (A) *The doctrine of the Ideal State.*

Concerning the authorship and source of this doctrine, there are two conclusions: First, Plato was not the author of the Republic and second, the allegory of the charioteer and winged steeds, is not a product of Plato, but is derived from the Egyptian Book of the Dead, in the Judgment Drama.

Concerning the first conclusion it is only necessary to re-affirm what has already been stated in connection with the writings of Plato, and that is that they are disputed not only by such modern scholars as Grote and Schaarsmidt, but also by ancient historians: Diogenes Laertius, Aristoxenus and Favorinus (80-150 A. D.), who declare that the subject matter of the Republic was found in the controversies written by Protagoras (481-411 B. C.) at the time of whose death Plato was but a boy.

Furthermore, the authorship of Plato rests only upon the opinions of Aristotle and Theophrastus, both of whose aims were the compilation of a Greek philosophy with Egyptian material.

(Diogenes Laertius, p. 311 and 327; Aristotle Metaphysics Bk. I).

(Zeller's History of Philosophy; Introduction, p. 8 and 13; Wm. Turner's History of Philosophy, p. 95).

Concerning the second conclusion, it must be pointed out that the allegory of the "Charioteer and the winged steeds" is a description of the quality and destiny of the soul as it appears at the bar of justice, in the Judgment Drama of the Egyptian Book of the Dead. In this Drama, the Great Chief Justice and President of the Unseen World, Pethempamenthes, i.e., Osiris is seated on a throne, and is attended by the Goddesses Isis and Nephthys, while 42 assistant judges are seated around.

Near Osiris there are four genii of Amenthe, the Unseen World, represented as short vases, called canopi, in which the different viscera, symbolizing the moral qualities of the individual, are kept embalmed. The intestines have a very important connection with the moral qualities of the individual since they are blamed for any sin which the individual commits. At the opposite end the deceased is introduced by Horus, while in the centre stands the Scale of Justice which has been erected by Anubis. On one side of it, there appears a heart-shaped vase containing the moral qualities of the deceased, while on the other side, there is a figure of the Goddess of Truth. Toth, the scribe, holding a roll of papyrus, stands by and makes a record of the weighing. After this is completed, Horus receives the record from Toth and advances to Osiris to make known the results. Osiris listens and at the end of the report, pronounces sentence of reward or punishment. In the meantime, fearful monsters lurk around the scene to destroy the soul, if the verdict is against it.

Let us observe that

(1) the motion of the scale in the Judgment Drama corresponds with the up and down motion of the winged steeds of the allegory

(2) the opposite qualities weighed on the scale correspond with the opposite qualities possessed by the noble and ignoble steeds of the allegory

(3) the idea of justice symbolized by the scale of Judgment Drama, corresponds with the idea of justice expressed in the allegory.

(4) The winged steeds corresponds with the monsters of the judgment drama.

(B) *The Authorship of the Republic.*

According to Diogenes Laertius book III and pages 311 and 327, it is stated both by Aristoxenus and Favorinus, that nearly the whole of the subject matter of Plato's Republic was found in the Controversies, written by Protagoras. Furthermore, according to Roger's Students History of Philosophy p. 78, it is stated that although Plato might have drawn heavily upon the reminiscences of Socrates, whose lectures he attended: yet the subject matter of the Republic is a more carefully reasoned system of philosophy, than can be easily attributed to Socrates. That the whole volume is a cumulative argument into which there are subtly interwoven opinions on almost every subject of philosophical importance.

It is obvious that modern scholarship doubts that Plato drew the subject matter of the Republic from

Socrates, and is inclined to attribute authorship to Plato himself. If however, we take into consideration the fact that the subject matter of the Republic was in circulation long before the time of Plato: for Protagoras is supposed to have lived from 481-411 B. C. and Plato, from 427-347 B. C., reason forbids the assignment of the authorship to Plato.

But the important question remains: From what source did Protagoras draw the ideas of the Republic which were circulated in the Controversies?

Text books on Greek philosophy tell us that Protagoras was a pupil of Democritus; but when we turn to the writings of Democritus we are unable to discover any connection between them and the (a) educational system and the (b) paternal government which are advocated in the Republic.

This fact forces us to the conclusion that the subject matter of Plato's Republic was neither produced by Plato, nor any Greek philosopher.

(C) *The Authorship of Timaeus.*

According also to Diogenes Laertius Book VIII p. 399-401, when Plato visited Dionysius at Sicily, he paid Philolaus, a Pythagorean, 40 Alexandrian Minae of silver, for a book, from which he copied the whole contents of the Timaeus.

Under these circumstances it is clear that Plato wrote neither the Republic nor the Timaeus, whose subject matter identifies them with the purpose of the Mysteries of Egypt.

(Roger's Students Hist. of Philosophy p. 76; 78; and 104).
(Zeller's Hist. of Philosophy: Introduction p. 13 and 103).
(Wm. Turner's Hist. of Philosophy p. 79 and 95).
(Plato; Apology, Crito, and Phaedo).
(Xenophon: Memorabilia; Strabo; Ancient Mysteries by C. H. Vail).
(Clement: Stromata Bk. V. C. 7 and 9).

VI. *The Chariot was not a culture pattern of the Greeks, at the time of Plato, nor was it used by them in warfare:-*

Greek culture and traditions did not furnish Plato with the idea of the chariot and winged steeds, for nowhere in their brief military history, (i.e., up to the time of Plato) do we find the use of such a war machine by the Greeks.

The only nearby nation who specialized in the manufacture of chariots and the breeding of horses was the Egyptians. When Joseph was Governor in Egypt, the horse and war chariot were in use; and when the Israelites fled from the country, Pharaoh pursued them to the Red Sea in chariots. Even Homer and Diodorus who visited Egypt, testify that they saw a great multitude of war chariots and numerous stables along the banks of the Nile, from Memphis to Thebes.

And since the Judgment Drama in the Egyptian Book of the Dead reveals the entire philosophy contained in the allegory, Plato cannot be credited as its author.

The following sketch of the military history of the Greeks shows that the chariot was not used by them, nor was it their culture pattern:-

A. *Exernal wars or wars with the Persians.*

(a) *The Ionian revolt against Persian rule, 499-494 B. C.*
   This climaxed in a naval engagement at Lade, where the Ionian fleet was defeated.

(b) *The batle of Marathon, 490 B. C.*
   During the summer of 490 B. C., the Greeks met the Persians at the bay of Marathon, and after a brief fight with bows and arrows, both belligerents withdrew to prepare for more decisive engagements.

(c) *The battle of Thermopylae, 480 B. C.*
   Ten years after Marathon, the Persians and Greeks met again to settle their grievances. The Persians anchored in the Gulf of Pagasae, while the Greeks anchored off Cape Artimesium. A battle followed and Thermopylae was captured by the Persians.

(d) *The battle of Salamis, 479 B. C.*

Both Persians and Greeks met again at Salamis in 479 B. C., and a naval engagement followed, with considerable loss of ships on both sides. Both belligerents withdrew without any decision.

(e) *The confederacy of Delos and their wars with the Persians, 478-448 B. C.*

The purpose of the confederacy was defense against Persian aggression, and two naval battles were fought: one at the river Eurymedon in 467 B. C., when the Greeks gained a minor victory, and the other at Cyprus in 449 B. C., when the island was captured by the Persians.

N. B.

Chariots were not used in any of these engagements.

B. *Internal wars, i.e., the Peloponnesian wars, 460-445 B. C., and 431-421 B. C. respectively.*

These wars were fought between the different Greek states, and their major engagements were maritime.

In 432 B. C. Athens blockaded Potidaea and Megara was excluded from Greek markets. In 431 B. C. Thèbes attacked Plataea, and while a Peloponnesian army occupied Attica, an Athenian fleet raided Peloponnesus.

Pericles conducted the evacuation of Attica, the oligarchs at Corcyra were massacred, and after the seizure of Amphipolis; Nicias sued for peace 422 B. C.

N. B.

It is evident that Greek culture and tradition did not furnish Plato with the idea of the charioteer and winged steeds, for nowhere in their brief military history, (i.e., up to the time of Plato) do we find the use of such a war machine by the Greeks as a chariot. The only nearby nation who specialized in the manufacture of chariots and horse breeding was the Egyptians, as already mentioned.

And since the Judgment Drama in the Egyptian Book of

the Dead depicts the allegory of the charioteer and winged
steeds, credit for its authorship cannot be given to Plato, but
to the Egyptians.

(Sandford: Mediterranean World, c. 12, p. 197; 202; 203;
205; c. 13, p. 220-221).
(Genesis, c. 45, 27; c. 47, 17; Deut. c. 17, 16).
(I Kings, c. 10, 28).
(Homer II. i, 381; Diodorus; Roger's Hist. of Phil., p. 83-
84).
(John Kendrick: Ancient Egypt, Vol. I, p. 166).
(The Egyptian Book of the Dead).

3. **Aristotle: (i) (a) Early Life and Training and (b)
His Own List of Books (c) Other Lists of Books (ii)
Doctrines (iii) Summary of Conclusions: A. His Doc-
trines B. (i) The Library of Alexandria B. (ii) True
Source of his Unusual Number of Books C. The Dis-
crepancies and Doubts in His Life.**

(i) (a) *Birth and early life and training.*

According to the textbooks on the history of Greek philosophy, Aristotle was born in 384 B. C. at Stagira, a town in
Thrace. His father, Neomachus is said to have been a physi-
cian to Amyntas, King of Macedonia. Nothing is mentioned
in books about his early education, only that he became an
orphan and at the age of 19 he went to Athens, where he
spent twenty years as a pupil of Plato.

We are also informed that after the death of Plato, his
nephew, became the master of his school, and that Aristotle
left immediately for Mysia, where he met and married the
niece of Hermeias.

Likewise, that after the death of Amyntas of Macedon, his
son Phillip having become king, appointed Aristotle as Tutor
of his son Alexander a boy of 13 years (later to be called the
Great in consequence of his conquest of Egypt).

After Phillip's assassination in 336 B. C. Alexander became

king, and we are informed that he immediately planned an
Asiatic campaign and included Egypt, during which time Aristotle is said to have returned to Athens and founded a school
in a gymnasium called the Lyceum. We are further informed
that Aristotle conducted this school for only twelve years, that
Alexander the Great advanced him the funds to purchase a
large number of books, that his pupils were called Peripatetics,
and that owing to an indictment for impiety, brought against
him by a priest named Eurymedon, he fled from Athens to
Chalcis in Euboea, where he remained in exile until his death
in 322 B. C.

> (Roger's Student's History of Phil. p. 104).
> (Zeller's History of Philosophy, p. 171-172).
> (Fuller's History of Philosophy, Aristotle's Life).
> (B. D. Alexander's Hist. of Phil. p. 91-92).
> (Diogenes Laertius Bk. V. p. 449).

(b) *His own list of books.*

Aristotle is credited with classifying his own writings as
follows:-

(i) The Theoretic, whose object is truth, and which included (a) Mathematics (b) Physics and (c) Theology.

(ii) The Practical, whose object is the useful, and which
included (a) Ethics (b) Economics and (c) Politics.

(iii) The Productive or Poetic whose object is the beautiful,
and which included (a) Poetry (b) Art and (c) Rhetoric.

N. B.

Neither Logic nor Metaphysics was in this list.

(History of Philosophy, B. D. Alexander, p. 92).

(c) *Other lists of books.*

There are two lists of books which have come down to modern times from Alexandrine and Arabian sources.

(i) The older list, derived from the Alexandrine Hermippus
(200 B. C.), who estimated the books of Aristotle at 400,
which, according to Zeller's suggestion, must have been in

the Alexandrine Library, at the time of the compilation of the list, since works which are now considered to be Aristotle's are not found in the list.

(ii) The later, derived from Arabian sources, was compiled by Ptolemus, of the First or Second Century A. D. This list mentions most of the works in the modern collection, and has a total of one thousand books.

(Zeller's History of Philosophy, p. 172-173; B. D. Alexander's History of Philosophy, p. 92-93).

(ii) DOCTRINES OF ARISTOTLE

I. *Metaphysics: or The Principles of Being, in the Metaphysical realm.*

1. Aristotle defines Metaphysics as the science of Being as Being.

2. He names the Attributes of Being as
   (a) actuality (*entelecheia*) i.e., perfection and
   (b) potentiality i.e., the capacity for perfection. (*dynamis*).

3. He states that all created beings are composed of actuality and potentiality.

These two principles are present and are mixed in all created beings except one, whose being is actuality, and includes the composition of (a) matter and form (b) substance and accident (c) soul and its faculties (d) active and passive intellect.

II. *Principles of being in the physical realm.*

There are four principles of being in the physical realm which are called Causes:-

(1) Matter (*hyle*) the material cause, is the potentiality or capacity of existence (*hyle prote*). It is that out of which being is made.

(2) Form or Essence (*morphe*) i.e., the formal cause is that which gives actuality to existence. It is that into which a thing is made. When matter is united with form the result is organized or realized being that has come to existence in the processes of nature (*synolon, ousia prote*).

(3) Final Cause, is that for which everything exists. Everything has a purpose and that purpose is the final cause. A final cause always implies intelligence: but this is not always true in the case of the efficient Cause.

Consequently in the realm of nature, every being or living organism is the complex effect of four causes:-

(1) The substance out of which it is made (i.e., material cause).

(2) The type or idea, according to which the embryo tends to develop (i.e., formal cause).

(3) The act of creation or generation (i.e., efficient cause).

(4) The purpose or end for which the organism is created (i.e., final cause). In other words, matter, type, creation and purpose are the four principles which underlie all existing things.

(B. D. Alexander's History of Philosophy, p. 97-100; Aristotle, Meta. I, 3; Wm. Turner's History of Philosophy, p. 136-140. Alfred Weber's Hist. of Phil., p. 80-84).

III. *Doctrines concerning the existence of God.*

(1) Although motion is eternal, there cannot be an indefinite series of movers and the moved, therefore there must be One, the first in the series which is unmoved (*proton kinoun akineton*) i.e., The Unmoved Mover.

(2) The actual is antecedent to the potential for although last in appearance, is really first in nature. Therefore before all matter and the composition of actual and potential, pure actuality must have existed. Therefore actuality is the cause of all things that exist and since it is pure actuality, its life is essentially free from all material conditions. It is the thought of thought, the absolute spirit, who dwells in eternal peace and self enjoyment, who knows himself and the absolute truth, and is in need of neither action nor virtue.

(3) God is one, for matter is the principle of plurality, and the First Intelligence is free from material conditions. His life is contemplative thought: neither providence nor will is

comparable with the eternal repose in which He dwells. God is not concerned with the world.

IV. *The doctrine of the origin of the world.*

The world is eternal, because matter, motion and time are eternal.

V. *The doctrine concerning Nature.*

Nature is everything which has the principle of motion and rest. It is spontaneous and self determining from within. Nature does nothing in vain, but according to definite law. It is always striving for the best according to a plan of development, which is obstructed only by matter. The striving of nature is through the less perfect to the more perfect.

VI. *The doctrine concerning the Universe.*

The world is globe shaped, circular and most perfect in form. The heaven, which is composed of ether, stands in immediate contact with the First Cause. The stars, which are eternal come next in order, the earth-ball is in the middle, and is the furthest from the prime mover, and least participant of divinity.

(Eth. Wic 10, 8; 1178b, 20) (Op. cit. 10: 8, 9; 1179).

(Wm. Turner's History of Philosophy, p. 141-143; B D. Alexander, History of Phil. p. 102-103; Zeller's History of Philosophy, p. 221; Roger's History of Philosophy, p. 109).

(Aristotle's Physics II, I, 192b 14) (De Caelo, I, 4, 271a, 33).

(De Part. An. IV, 2, 677a 15) (Aristotle's Physics II, 8, 199).

(B. D. Alexander's Hist. of Phil. p. 104).

(De Generatione Animalium, IV, 4, 770b, 9).

VII. *The doctrine of the soul.*

The soul is not merely a harmony of the body or the blending of opposites. It is neither the four elements nor their compound, for it transcends all material conditions.

The soul and body are not two distinct things: but one in two different aspects, i.e., just as form is related to matter.

The soul is the power which a living body possesses, and it is the end for which the body exists, i.e., the final cause of its existence.

While the soul which is the radical principle of life, is one, yet it has several faculties. Those faculties are:- (1) Sensitive (2) Rational (3) Nutritive (4) Appetitive (5) Locomotive.

Of these, the sensitive and the rational are the most important: sensation being the faculty by means of which the forms of sensible things are received, just as impression is made as by a seal; and intelligent knowledge being the faculty by means of which intellectual knowledge is acquired.

It is the seat of ideas only, it does not create them, since knowledge comes through the senses.

(B. D. Alexander's History of Philosophy, p. 105-106).

(Wm. Turner's History of Philosophy, p. 147-153).

(Zeller's History of Philosophy, p 201-204).

(iii) SUMMARY OF CONCLUSIONS.

A. *His Doctrines.*

1. *The doctrine of Being (To on).*

By declaring the attributes of Being as (a) actuality or the determining principle, and (b) potentiality or the indeterminate principle: Aristotle attempted to explain Reality in terms of the principle of opposites.

But this principle was used not only by the Pythagoreans, Parmenides, and Democritus in a similar manner but also by Socrates in his attempt to prove the immortality of the soul, and by Plato who saw reality as the concept of things as distinguished from the things themselves: as the noumena as distinct from phenomena, and as the real, distinct from the unreal.

But the principle of opposites originated from the Egyptian Mystery System, whose Gods were male and female, and whose temples carried in front of them two pillars as symbols of the principle of opposites. It is obvious that Aristotle was not the author of this doctrine, but the Egyptians.

(Aristotle's Metaphysics I, 5, 985b, 24; Aristotle's Metaphysics I, 5, 98b, 31).

(Aristotle's Metaphysics I, 6, 987b, 9; Wm. Turner's Hist. of Phil., p. 41; 47; 48).

(Plato's Phaedo, c. 15; c. 16 and c. 49; Parmenides 132D).

(Memphite Theology, King-ship and the Gods, by Frankfort, c. 3, p. 25, 26, 35).

(Egyptian Religion by Frankfort, p. 64, 73, 88).

2. *The existence of God.*

(a) The teleological concept has not only been embraced by Socrates, Plato and Aristotle, but also by the peoples of the remotest antiquity. In the accounts found in the first chapter of Genesis and in the Memphite Theology, found in chapters 20 and 23 of Frankfort's Ancient Egyptian Religion, creation proceeds from chaos to order, by definite and gradual steps, showing design and purpose in nature, and suggesting that it must be the work of a divine Intelligence. The dates of these sources carry us far back into antiquity, many centuries before the time of Aristotle, between 2000 and 5000 B. C.

We are also told that in addition to the teleological concept, Aristotle introduced the concept of the "Unmoved Mover" in order to prove the existence of God. But the "Unmoved Mover" is none other than the Atum of the Memphite Theology of the Egyptians, the Demiurge, through whose command (*logos*) four pairs of Gods were created out of different parts of his body and who accordingly moved out of him. This act of creation took place while Atum remained unmoved, as he embraced Ptah. Thus the family of Nine Gods was created, and has been named the Ennead. It is quite clear that the concept of the "Unmoved Mover" is derived from the Egyptian theological or mystery system, and not from Aristotle, as the modern world has been made to believe.

[118]

N. B.

Incidentally, but no less important, it might be mentioned here that in this story of the created Gods by Atum the Sun God into a family of nine, i.e., the Ennead, we have the original source of two important scientific hypotheses of modern times:-

(1) There are nine major planets and (2) The Sun is the parent of the other planets (This latter being supported by the Nebular Hypothesis). Let us remember also that

(a) the worship of the planets began in Egypt and

(b) the Egyptian temples were the first observatories of history.

(c) In attempting to prove the existence of God or a First Cause by reference to actuality and potentiality, Aristotle simply followed the traditional custom of the Ancients, who used the principle of Opposites in order to explain the functions of nature.

(d) Plato used it, through the theory of Ideas, to explain the real and unreal in the phenomena of nature.

(e) Socrates used it in order to establish the fact of immortality by showing that the death of one form of life of existing things, is but the beginning of another form of life of these things. In other words life is perpetual, it only changes its form in its course of progress.

Democritus applied the principle of opposites in their interpretation of a particular phase of reality. We cannot therefore consider Aristotle's use of the terms, actuality and potentiality in the problem of the existence of God as a new method of interpretation.

Furthermore, Aristotle's review of the doctrines of all previous philosophers including Plato, together with his exposure of their errors, and inconsistencies, shows that he had become confident not only of the fact that he was in possession of a new and correct knowledge one that had not before been made available to the Greeks, but also that he could then speak with

great authority. Right here I must say that I am convinced that
Aristotle represents a culture gap of 5000 years or more between his innovation and the Greek level of civilization; because it is impossible to escape the conviction that he obtained
his education and books from a nation outside of Greece, the
Egyptians who were far in advance of the culture of Greeks of
his day.

(Memphite Theology in Kingship & The Gods by Frankfort c. 3. p. 25, 26, 35).

(Herodotus I, 6-26) (Egyptian Religion by Frankfort p. 64,
73, 88).

(Plato's Phaedo c. 15, 16, 49) (Zeller's History of Philosophy p. 61).

(Aristotle's Eth., Nic. 10, 8; 1178b, 20) (Op. cit. 10: 8,
9; 1179).

(Zeller's History of Philosophy p. 221) (Roger's History of
Philosophy p. 109).

(William Turner's History of Philosophy p. 141-143).

(B. D. Alexander's History of Philosophy, p. 102, 103).

(B. D. Alexander's History of Philosophy p. 92, 93; Roger's
Student History of Philosophy p. 104).

(William Turner's History of Philosophy p. 126-127, 135).

(Zeller's History of Philosophy p. 171-173) (Plutarch's
Alexander) (Aristotle's Metaphysics) (William Turner's History of Philosophy, p. 128 footnote also Noct. Mt. 20: 5).

(Strabo).

3. *The doctrine of the origin of the world.*

According to the doctrine that has been ascribed to Aristotle:
"because matter, motion and time are eternal, therefore the
world is also eternal", he plainly accepts and repeats a doctrine
which has also been ascribed to Democritus (400 B. C.), whose
dictum we are all quite familiar with: ex nihillo nihil fit
(nothing comes out of nothing), and consequently matter or
the world must always have existed.

But the antiquity of the doctrine of the eternal nature of

matter, takes us back to the creation story of the Memphite Theology of the Egyptians, in which Chaos is represented by the Primeval Ocean Nun, out of which there arose the Primeval Hill Ta-tjenen. Under these circumstances we cannot give Aristotle credit for the authorship of this doctrine.

In addition to the false authorship that has been attributed to Aristotle, he contradicts himself in his physics VIII 1. 25; when he also speaks of the world as caused. A thing cannot be eternal and infinite, and at the same time finite.

(Memphite Theology in Egyptian Religion by Frankfort p. 20).
(Intellectual Adventure of Man by Frankfort p. 10, 21, 52).

4. *The doctrine of the attributes of nature.*

Aristotle defines nature as that which possesses the principle of motion and rest and also adds that the motion is an effort to move from the less perfect to the more perfect by a definite law: supposedly what we would today call evolution.

As we examine this definition, we find that Aristotle has only applied the principle of opposites to explain one of the modes by which nature has revealed herself just as he has done in his attempt to explain Being in the dual terms of actuality and potentiality.

But change and motion, permanence and rest, were by no means new problems at the time of Aristotle; since they appear to have been investigated not only by Parmenides, Zeno and Melissus, but also by Democritus, who stressed the notion of permanence in his famous dictum: ex nihillo nihil fit (out of nothing, nothing comes) implying thereby that nature is permanent and eternal.

Similarly, his reference to nature's movement from the less perfect to the more perfect, was by no means a new discovery of a principle of nature.

The creation account found in the first chapter of Genesis speaks of the gradual development of life, in which the Demiurge or Logos was engaged at work during six stages and re:ed on the seventh. Similarly, the creation account of the Egyptians found in the Memphite Theology, also speaks of nature's movement from Chaos to order.

These accounts by many thousand years antedate Aristotle's time for the former is about 2000 B. C. while the latter 4000 B. C., and since the principle of opposites has already been shown to originate from the Egyptians, as well as that of the gradual development of life, it is clear that this doctrine on the attributes of nature did not originate from Aristotle.

(Zeller's History of Philosophy, p. 60-65;) (William Turner's History of Philosophy p. 44-52).
(Genesis c. 1).
(Roger's History of Philosophy p. 28-32).
(Intellectual Adventure of Man by Frankfort, p. 21, 51-60).
(Ancient Egyptian Religion by Frankfort, p. 20, 23).

5. *The Soul.*

According to Aristotle the soul possesses the following attributes (1) Identity with body, as form with matter (2) The power which a living body possesses, i.e., the radical principle of life, manifesting itself in the following attributes:-

(a) sensitive
(b) rational
(c) nutritive
(d) appetitive
(e) locomotive.

This description of the soul by Aristotle, seems to vary somewhat from the more familiar and current ideas held by the Atomists, on the one hand and Socrates, Plato and the Pythagoreans on the other; for while the former believed that the soul is material and is composed of fire atoms; the latter regarded it as a harmony of the body and a blending of opposites.

(William Turner's History of Philosophy, p. 42, 67-68).

[122]

(Plato Phaedo, c. 15) (Zeller's History of Philosophy, p. 61).

(De Respiratione, 4, 30, 47a).

Naturally we are now forced to ask the question: Did this doctrine of the soul originate from Aristotle? It is clear that he did not get it from his teacher Plato, nor from the Pythagoreans and Atomists; but from some other source outside of Greece.

As we turn our attention to ancient history, we happily discover that there are two such sources outside of Greece (1) The Creation story in Genesis first chapter and (2) The Egyptian Book of the Dead, which does not only contain attributes of the soul, identical with those mentioned by Aristotle, but far more in an elaborate system of philosophy in which human nature is explained as a unity of nine inseparable parts consisting of different bodies and souls interdependent one upon another, the physical body being one of them. (The Egyptian Book of the Dead by Sir E. A. Budge. Introduction, p. 29-64).

In the Genesis story, it is asserted that God made man out of matter (i.e., the dust of the earth), and breathed into his nostrils, the breath of life, and "man became a living soul". Here we have a clear statement of the identity of "body and soul", taken from a document (Genesis) which antedates Aristotle by many centuries.

In the Egyptian Book of the Dead, we also find that the human soul is composed of the following nine inseparable parts:-

(1) The Ka, which is an abstract personality of the man to whom it belongs possessing the form and attributes of a man with power of locomotion, omnipresence and ability to receive nourishment like a man. It is equivalent to (*Eidolon*), i.e., image.

(2) The Khat, i.e., the concrete personality, the physical body, which is mortal.

(3) The Ba, i.e., the heart-soul, which dwells in the Ka and

sometimes alongside it, in order to supply it with air and food. It has the power of metamorphosis and changes its form at will.

(4) The Ab, i.e., the Heart, the animal life in man, and is rational, spiritual and ethical. It is associated with the Ba (heart-soul) and in the Egyptian Judgment Drama it undergoes examination in the presence of Osiris, the great Judge of the Unseen World.

(5) The Kaibit, i.e., shadow. It is associated with Ba (heart-soul) from whom like the Ka, it receives its nourishment. It has the power of locomotion and omnipresence.

(6) The Khu, i.e., spiritual soul, which is immortal. It is also closely associated with the Ba (heart-soul), and is an Ethereal Being.

(7) The Sahu, i.e., spiritual body, in which the Khu or spiritual soul dwells. In it all the mental and spiritual attributes of the natural body are united to the new powers of its own nature.

(8) The Sekhem, i.e., power or the spiritual personification of the vital force in a man. Its dwelling place is in the heavens with spirits or Khus.

(9) The Ren, i.e., the name, or the essential attribute for the preservation of a Being. The Egyptians believed that in the absence of a name, an individual ceased to exist.

N. B.

It must be noted that according to the Egyptian concept

(1) The soul has nine parts, whose unity is so complete, that even the Ren, i.e., the name, is an essential attribute, since without it, it cannot exist.

(2) The Ba (or heart-soul), is connected with the Ka, Kaibit and Ab (Abstract personality or Shadow and Animal life) on the one hand, and also with Khu and Sekhem (spiritual Soul and spiritual personification of vital force) on the other hand, as the power of Nourishment.

[124]

(3) The Sahu is a spiritual body which is used both by Khu and Sekhem.

(4) The Khat, i.e., the physical body, is essential to the soul while manifesting itself upon the physical plane.

(5) The soul has the additional following attributes:-
    (a) omnipresence
    (b) metamorphosis
    (c) locomotion
    (d) nutritive
    (e) mortality (in case ᴏ. ᴛne khat)
    (f) immortality
    (g) rationality
    (h) spirituality
    (i) morality
    (j) ethereal
    (k) shadowy

(6) It is clear therefore from such a comparison as this, that the Aristotelian doctrine of the soul is identical and coincides with only a very small portion of the Egyptian philosophy of the soul, which therefore stands in relation to it as a whole to its part. Consequently we must conclude that Aristotle obtained his doctrine of the soul from the Egyptian Book of the Dead, directly or indirectly.

B (i) *The Library of Alexandria was the true source of Aristotle's large numbers of books:*

It is to be expected that the library of Alexandria was immediately ransacked and looted by Alexander and his party, no doubt made up of Aristotle and others, who did not only carry off large quantities of scientific books: but also frequently returned to Alexandria for the purpose of research. Just as these books were captured in Egypt by the army of Alexander and fell into the hands of Aristotle, so after Aristotle's death, these very books were destined to be captured by a Roman army and conveyed to Rome according to the following story taken from the histories of Strabo and Plutarch:-

The books of Aristotle fell into the hands of Theophrastus who succeeded him as Head of his School. At the death of Theophrastus, they were bequeathed to Neleus of Scepsis. After the death of Neleus, the books were hidden in a cellar, where they remained for almost two centuries.

When Athens was captured by the Romans in 84 B. C., the books were captured by Sulla and carried to Rome, where Tyrannio a grammarian secured copies and enabled Andronicus of Rhodes to publish them.

(Strabo; Plutarch; Wm. Turner's Hist. of Phil., p. 128 footnote).

(Noct., Mt, 20; 5)

The fragmentary character of Aristotle's writings and their lack of unity, reveal the fact that he himself made notes hurriedly from books while doing his research at the great Egyptian Library. The ancient teaching method was oral; not by lecture and note taking.

Right here I must repeat that I am convinced that Aristotle represents a culture gap of 5000 years between his innovation and the Greek level of civilization; because it is impossible to escape the conviction that he obtained his education and books from a nation outside of Greece, who was far ahead of the culture of the Greeks of his day, and that was the Egyptians.

(B. D. Alexander's History of Philosophy, p. 92 and 93).
(Roger's Student History of Philosophy, p. 104).
(Alfred Weber's History of Philosophy, p. 77 and 78).
(Wm. Turner's History of Philosophy, p. 126, 127, 135).
(Zeller's History of Philosophy, p. 171-173).
(Plutarch's Alexander, c. 8).
(Aristotle's Metaphysics) (Wm. Turner's History of Phil., p. 128 footnote also Noct., Mt., 20; 5).
(Strabo).

The so-called books of Aristotle deal with scientific knowledge which was not in circulation among the Greeks, and

[126]

consequently, it was impossible, as has already been stated, for him to have purchased them from other so-called Greek philosophers.

It is for the purpose of concealing the true source of his books and of his education, that history tells the very strange stories about Aristotle (a) that he spent 20 years, as a pupil under Plato, whom we know was incompetent to teach him; and (b) that Alexander the Great also gave him money to buy the large number of books to which his name has been attached; but at the same time, fails to tell us when, where and from whom Aristotle bought the books.

Furthermore, as already pointed out, Aristotle's review of the doctrines of all previous philosophers including Plato, together with his exposure of their errors and inconsistencies, shows that he had become confident not only of the fact that he was in possession of correct knowledge, one that had not before been made available to the Greeks; but also that he could then speak with great authority.

B (ii) *The lack of uniformity between the lists of books points to doubtful authorship.*

1. There are at least three lists of books. One list is said to be Aristotle's own classification of his writings, and naturally it must be dated within the period of his own life time 384-322 B. C. In this list Aristotle has told the world that he wrote texts on (a) Mathematics, Physics and Theology, (b) Ethics, Economics and Politics and (c) Poetry, Art and Rhetoric.

Now, in order to write these texts one must have received his education and training in the subjects on which they are written. We are told in the history of Greek philosophy, that Socrates taught Plato and that Plato taught Aristotle. But there is no evidence that Socrates ever taught mathematics or economics or politics.

Consequently, it was impossible for him to teach Plato these subjects, and also impossible for Plato to teach Aristotle these subjects, under the Egyptian Mystery System which was graded, and which required proof of efficiency before promotion.

We are therefore unable to accept the claim of Aristotle to have been the author of those books.

2. Two lists are derived from different sources and the two together differ widely in (a) number (b) subject matter and (c) date.

The list of Hermippus the Alexandrine (200 B. C.) contains 400 books. The list compiled by Ptolemus, between First and Second Centuries A. D. contains 1000 books. The very fact that there is no uniformity in the lists points to a doubtful authorship. Also, if Aristotle in 200 B. C. had only 400 books, by what miracle did they increase to 1000 in the Second Century A. D.? Or was it forgery?

C. *The discrepancies and doubts in his life.*

(i) *He wastes 20 years as a pupil under Plato:-*

It is said that he went to Plato at the age of 19 and spent 20 years with him as a pupil. But this is doubtful and unreasonable. Doubtful because Plato is regarded as a Philosopher, while Aristotle as a Scientist, who has been credited with all the scientific knowledge of the Ancient World, and it is impossible for a master to teach a pupil what he himself does not know.

It is also unreasonable to expect a man who has been credited with Aristotle's knowledge, to waste 20 of the best years of his life, under a master who was incompetent to teach him.

(B. D. Alexander, Hist. of Phil., p. 92; Roger's Student History of Philosophy, p. 104).

(ii) *The truth of how he got such a large number of books is misrepresented:-*

He is said to have received financial aid from Alexander the Great, and was able to purchase a large number of books in order to advance his studies.

(Zeller's Hist. of Phil., p. 171; Wm. Turner's History of Phil. p. 127).

But this sounds more like a fable than the truth, for up to the time of Aristotle, Greek education was represented by the Sophists who taught Rhetoric and dialectics; while the study of elementary science was confined to a few unknown philosophers. This was the standard of Greek education, for the Sophists were the only authorized teachers.

Yet Aristotle is credited with producing a thousand different books dealing with all branches of the scientific knowledge of antiquity. Certainly he could not have obtained them from the Greeks, for that vast body of knowledge, which bears his name and which was presented as new, would really have been the traditional common possession of all who were members of the Greek schools of philosophy for they would have been the only persons inside Greece permitted to own such books; for knowledge was protected as secret.

Under these circumstances it is evident that the vast body of scientific knowledge ascribed to Aristotle, was neither in the possession of the Greeks of his time, nor was there any one in Greece competent to teach him Science and, least of all, on so vast a scale.

(iii) *He got the books by looting the Library of Alexandria*:-

The question must now be asked: How did Aristotle, a single individual, come to possess such a vast number of scientific works, a body of knowledge which took the Ancient World five thousand years or more to accumulate? It is evident that Aristotle's fame as a scholar has been grossly exaggerated: for such an accomplishment would have been both a physical and mental impossibility. Throughout the intellectual advancement of man, the world has witnessed many a genius; but those have always been specialists in particular fields, not specialists in every branch of science.

And the modern world is no exception, for our great men

of science are not specialists in every branch of science, but only in a particular one. That appears to be nature's way.

As a matter of fact, the many discrepancies and doubts in the life and activities of Aristotle lead us to the only reasonable solution of the problem that instead of the tales (a) that Alexander the Great gave him money to buy books (b) that he spent 20 years of his life as a pupil with Plato and (c) that he left the Palace of Alexander for Athens, when Alexander started on his Egyptian invasion, he, on the contrary, must have spent a large part of those 20 years under the tutorship of the Egyptian Priests, and also must have accompanied Alexander on the Egyptian invasion, which gave him the opportunity, not only to carry away from the Alexandrian Library, the vast number of books which are now said to be his, but also to copy notes from a large number of volumes. Indeed modern scholarship has shown that the writings of Aristotle bear all the marks of hurriedly copied notes which of course suggests that Aristotle himself copied these notes from the books of the Alexandrian Library. The historical account of Aristotle's life is incredible.

(iv) *It was the custom of ancient armies to capture books as valuable war booty*:-

When a victorious army takes possession of a country, it is customary for special companies to search for and sieze war booty, i.e., to help themselves to everything that is considered valuable. The Greeks, among all the surrounding nations, were the most anxious to obtain the valuable secrets of the Egyptians, in the Ancient Sciences, and it would appear that the greatest opportunity came to them to accomplish the desire when Alexander the Great invaded Egypt. As stated elsewhere, ancient invading armies looted libraries, because of the great value attached to books; and temples were also looted, not only for books, but also for the gold and silver, out of which the gods and ceremonial vessels were made.

CHAPTER VII:

The Curriculum of the Egyptian Mystery System.

1. The Education of the Egyptian Priests According to Their Orders.

From Diodorus, Herodotus and Clement of Alexandria, we learn that there were six Orders of Egyptian Priests, and that each Order had to master a certain number of the books of Hermes. Clement has described a procession of the Priests, calling them by their Order, and stating their qualifications, as follows:

First comes the Singer Odus, bearing an instrument of music. He has to know by heart two of the books of Hermes; one containing the hymns of the Gods, and the other, the allotment of the king's life. Next comes the Horoscopus, carrying in his hand a horologium or sun-dial, and a palm branch; the symbols of Arstronomy. He has to know four of the books of Hermes, which deal with Astronomy.

Next comes the Hierogrammat, with feathers on his head, and a book in his hand, and a rectangular case with writing materials, i.e., the writing ink and the reed. He has to know the hieroglyphics, cosmography, geography, astronomy, the topography of Egypt, the sacred utensils and measures, the temple furniture and the lands.

Next comes the Stolistes, carrying the cubit of justice, and the libation vessels. He has to know the books of Hermes that deal with the slaughter of animals.

Next comes the Prophetes carrying the vessel of water, followed by those who carry the loaves.

The Prophetes is the President of the temple and has to know the ten books which are called hieratic, and contain the laws and doctrines concerning the Gods (secret-theology) and the whole education of the Priests. The books of Hermes are 42 in number and are absolutely necessary. 36 of them have to be known by the Orders which precede, and contain the whole philosophy of the Egyptians.

The remaining six books must be known by the Order of Pastophori. These are medical books and deal with physiology, male and female diseases, anatomy, drugs and instruments. The books of Hermes were well known to the ancient world and were known to Clement of Alexandria, who lived at the beginning of the third century A. D.

In addition to the education contained in the 42 Books of Hermes, the Priests gained considerable knowledge from the selection and examination of sacrificial victims, and the strict bodily purity which their priestly office imposed.

In addition to the Hierogrammat and Horoscopus, who were skilled in theology and hieroglyphics, a Priest was also a Judge and an interpreter of the law. This led to a select tribunal, which made the Egyptian Priest the custodian of every kind of literature. We are also told that the Science of Statistics was cultivated to the greatest perfection among the Egyptian Priests.

(Diodorus I, 80; Clement of Alexandria; Stromata 6, 4, p. 756; John Kendrick's Ancient Egypt Bk. I, p. 378-379; Bk. II, 85-87; Aelian, Var. Hist. 14, 34; Clement of Alexandria: Stromata 6, 4, p 758: John Kendrick's Ancient Egypt Bk. II p. 31-33).

2. The Education of the Egyptian Priests in—A. The Seven Liberal Arts. B. Secret Systems of Languages and Mathematical Symbolism. C. Magic.

A. *The education of the Egyptian Priests in the Seven Liberal Arts.*

As has already been pointed out, in connection with Plato and the Cardinal Virtues, the Egyptian Mysteries were the centre of organized culture, and the recognized source of education in the ancient world. Neophytes were graded according to their moral efficiency and intellectual competence, and had to submit to many years of tests and ordeals, in order that their eligibility for advancement might be determined. Their education included the Seven Liberal Arts, and the virtues. The virtues were not mere abstractions or ethical sentiments; but positive valours and the virility of the soul. Beyond these, the Priests entered upon a course of specialization.

B. *The education of the Egyptian Priests consisted also in the specialization in secret systems of language and mathematical symbolism.*

(i) It would appear that there were two forms of writing in use among the Egyptians: (a) The demotic, believed to have been introduced by Pharaoh Psammitichus, for trade and commercial purposes; and (b) The hieroglyphics of which there were two forms, i.e., the hieroglyphics proper, and the hieratic a linear form, both of which were used only by the Priests, in order to conceal the secret and mystical meaning of their doctrines. (Clement of Alexandria: Stromata Bk. V. c. 4 p. 657; Plutarch, De Iside et Osiride Bk. II, p. 374; John Kendrick; Ancient Egypt, Bk. II, p. 84; 119, 336, and 245).

(ii) We are also informed that the mystery system of Egypt employed modes of spoken language which could be understood, only by the initiated. These consisted not only of myths and parables; but also of a secret language called Senzar. (Ancient Mysteries: C. H. Vail, p. 23).

(iii) We also understand that the Egyptians attached numerical values both to letters of words and to geometrical figures, with the same intention as with their use of hieroglyphics, i.e., to conceal their teachings. It is further understood that the Egyptian numerical and geometrical symbolism were contained in the 42 Books of Hermes, whose system was the oldest and most elaborate repository of mathematical symbolism. Here again we are reminded of the source of the number philosophy of Pythagoras.

(Ancient Mysteries: C. H. Vail, p. 22-23; Clement of Alexandria: Stromata Book V, c. 7 and 9).

C. *The education of the Egyptian Priests consisted also in the specialization in magic.*

According to Herodotus, the Egyptian Priests possessed super-natural powers, for they had been trained in the esoteric philosophy of the Greater Mysteries, and were experts in Magic. They had the power of controlling the minds of men (hypnosis), the power of predicting the future (prophecy) and the power over nature, (i.e., the power of Gods) by giving commands in the name of the Divinity and accomplishing great deeds. Herodotus also tells us that the most celebrated Oracles of the ancient world were located in Egypt: Hercules at Canopis; Apollo at Apollinopolis Magna; Minerva at Sais; Diana at Bubastis; Mars at Papremis; and Jupiter at Thebes and Ammonium; and that the Greek Oracles were Egyptian imitations.

Here it might be well to mention that the Egyptian Priests were the first genuine Priests of history, who exercised control over the laws of nature. Here it might also be well to mention that the Egyptian Book of the Dead is a book of magical formulae and instructions, intended to direct the fate of the departed soul. It was the Prayer Book of the Mystery System of Egypt, and the Egyptian Priest received training in post mortem conditions and the methods of their verification. It must also be noted that Magic was applied religion, or primitive scientific method.

(The Egyptian Book of the Dead; Herodotus Bk. II 109, 177; Sandford's Mediterranean World, p. 27; 507; Definition of Magic, Frazier's Golden Bough).

3. **A Comparison of the Curriculum of the Egyptian Mystery System with the Lists of Books Attributed to Aristotle.**

[134]

A. *The Curriculum*

The Curriculum of the Egyptian Mystery System consisted of the following subjects:

(i) *The Seven Liberal Arts,* which formed the foundation training for all Neophytes and included: grammar, Arithmetic, Rhetoric and Dialectic (i.e., the Quadrivium) and Geometry, Astronomy and Music (i.e., the Trivium).

(ii) *The Sciences of the 42 Books of Hermes*

In addition to the foundation training prescribed for all Neophytes, those who sought Holy Orders, had to be versed in the books of Hermes and according to Clement of Alexandria, their orders and subjects were as follows:—

(a) The Singer or Odus, who must know two books of Hermes dealing with Music i.e., the hymns of the Gods.

(b) The Horoscopus, who must know four books of Hermes dealing with Astronomy.

(c) The Hierogrammat, who must know the hieroglyphics, cosmography, geography, astronomy and the topography of Egypt and Land Surveying.

(d) The Stolistes, who must know the books of Hermes that deal with slaughter of animals and the process of embalming.

(e) The Prophetes, who is the President of the temple, and must know ten books of Hermes dealing with higher esoteric theology and the whole education of priests.

(f) The Pastophori, who must know six books of Hermes, which are medical books, dealing with physiology, the diseases of male and female, anatomy, drugs and instruments.

(iii) *The Sciences of the Monuments* (Pyramids, Temples, Libraries, Obelisks, Phinxes, Idols) ;—

Architecture, masonry, carpentry, engineering, sculpture, metallurgy, agriculture, mining and forestry. Art (drawing and painting).

(iv) *The Secret Sciences*

Numerical symbolism, geometrical symbolism, magic, the book of the Dead, myths and parables.

(v) *The Social Order and Its Protection*

The Priests of Egypt were also Lawyers, Judges, officials of government, Business Men and Sailors and Captains. Hence, they must have been trained in Economics, Civics, Law, Government, Statistics, sensus taking, navigation, ship building, military science, the manufacture of chariots and horse breeding.

If we compare 3A wih 3B which immediately follows, we would discover that the curriculum of the Egyptian Mystery System covered a much wider range of scientific subjects than those of Aristotle's list, which it includes.

N. B.

Note also that The Seven Liberal Arts: The Quadrivium and Trivium originated from the Egyptian Mysteries.

(The Mechanical Triumphs of the Ancient Egyptians by F. M. Barber).

(The Book of the Foundation of Temples by Moret).

(A short history of Mathematics by W. W. R. Ball).

(The Problem of Obelisks by R. Engelbach).

(The Great Pyramid Its Divine Message by D. Davidson).

(History of Mathematics by Florian Cajori).

B. *Aristotle's list of books, prepared by himself.*

(1) Aristotle is said to have prepared a list of books in the following order (B. D. Alexander's Hist. of Phil. p. 97; Wm. Turner's Hist. of Phil. p. 129).

(i) *Theoretic* whose purpose was truth, and which included (a) Mathematics (b) Physics and (c) Theology.

(ii) *Practical,* whose purpose was usefulness, and which included (a) Ethics (b) Economics (c) Politics and

(iii) *Poetic or Productive,* whose purpose was beauty, and which included (a) Poetry (b) Art and (c) Rhetoric. An examination and comparison of 3 A. with 3 B. show that (a) The Curriculum of the Egyptian Mystery System included all the scientific and philosophic subjects credited to the authorship of Aristotle. (b) The books attributed to Aristotle's authorship cannot be dissociated from Egyptian origin, as elsewhere referred to, both through the plunder of the Royal Library of Alexandria and through research carried on at the centre by Aristotle himself. As has been mentioned elsewhere, the writings of Aristotle are disputed by modern scholarship (Wm. Turner's Hist. of Phil. p. 127) and I feel more justified in making the comparison between the curriculum of the Mystery System and the list said to be drawn up by Aristotle himself; rather than with the notorious list of one thousand books, whose subjects are nevertheless included under the curriculum of the Egyptian Mystery System.

(Zeller's Hist. of Phil. p. 173).

CHAPTER VIII:

The Memphite Theology is the Basis of all Important Doctrines in Greek Philosophy.

History and Description:

The Memphite Theology is an inscription on a stone, now kept in the British Museum. It contains the theological, cosmological and philosophical views of the Egyptians. It has already been referred to in my treatment of Plato's doctrines; but it must be repeated here to show its full importance as the basis of the entire field of Greek philosophy. It is dated 700 B. C., and bears the name of an Egyptian Pharaoh who stated that he had copied an inscription of his ancestors. This statement is verified by language and typical arrangement of the text, and therefore assigns the original date of the Memphite Theology to a very early period of Egyptian history, i.e., the time when the first Dynasties had made their new capital at Memphis: the city of the God Ptah, i.e., between 4000 and 3500 B. C. (Intellectual Adventure of Man by Frankfort, p. 55).

The Text:

This consists of three supplementary parts, each of which will be treated separately: both as regards its teachings and the identity in Greek philosophy.

Part I presents the Gods of Chaos. Part II presents the Gods of Order and arrangement in creation; and Part III presents the Primate of the Gods, or the God of Gods, through whose (*Logos*) creation was accomplished.

In Part I pre-creation or chaos is represented as follows:—

A. *Text of Part I*:

The Primate of the Gods Ptah, conceived in his heart, everything that exists and by His utterance created them all. He

[139]

is first to emerge from the primeval waters of Nun in the form of a Primeval Hill. Closely following the Hill, the God Atom also emerges from the waters and sits upon Ptah (the Hill). There remain in the waters four pairs of male and female gods (the Ogdoad, or unity of Eight-Gods), bearing the following names:-

(1) Nun and Naunet, i.e., the Primeval waters and the counter heaven.

(2) Huh and Hauhet, i.e., the boundless and its opposite:

(3) Kuk and Kauket, i.e., darkness and its opposite; and

(4) Amun, i.e., (Amon) and Amaunet, i.e., the hidden and its opposite.

(Egyptian Religion by Frankfort, p. 20; 23. Intellectual Adventure of Ancient Man by Frankfort, p. 21).

B. *The Philosophy of Part I*:

(1) Ptah has the following attributes: (a) The Primate of the Gods, i.e., The God of Gods (b) The *Logos*. Thought and creative utterance and power (Egyptian Religion by Frankfort, p. 23). (c) The God of Order and form (d) The Divine Artificer and Potter (Fire Philosophy by Swinburne Clymer; Jamblichus; Ancient Egypt by John Kendrick, Bk. I, p. 318; 339).

It must be noted that while the Sun God Atom sits upon Ptah the Primeval Hill He accomplishes the work of creation. But the Memphite Theology dates back to 4000 B. C., when it is believed the Greeks were unknown (Frankfort's Intellectual Adventure of Man, p. 5; 53; 55. The Book of the Dead, p. 17).

This arrangement in the Memphite Theology could only mean that the ingredients of the Primeval Chaos contained ten principles: four pairs of opposite principles, together with two other gods: Ptah representing Mind, Thought, and creative Utterance; while Atom joins himself to Ptah and acts as Demiurge and executes the work of creation. From such an arrangement in the cosmos we are in position to infer the following philosophies:-

(a) Water is the source of all things.

(b) Creation was accomplished by the unity of two creative principles: Ptah and Atom, i.e., the unity of Mind (nous) with Logos (creative Utterance).

(c) Atom was the Demiurge or Intermediate God in creation. He was also Sun God or Fire God.

(d) Opposite Principles control the life of the universe.

(e) The elements in creation were Fire (Atom), Water (Nun), Earth (Ptah or Ta-tjenen) and Air.

Part I of the Memphite Theology is the correct Source of these philosophies: but strangely the Greeks have claimed them as their production, although without any right whatever.

C. Individual Greek Philosophers to whom portions of the philosophy of the Memphite Theology has been assigned:

Of these doctrines, "water as the source of all things" has been assigned to Thales (Zeller: Hist. of Phil. p. 38); that of the "Boundless or Unlimited", has been assigned to Anaximander (Zeller: Hist. of Phil. p. 40); while that of "Air as the basis of life" has been assigned to Anaximenes (Zeller: Hist. of Phil. p. 42). Furthermore, the doctrine "that Fire underlies the life of the universe", has been assigned not only to Pythagoras, who spoke of the functions of the central and peripheral Fires; but also to Heraclitus who spoke of the transmutation of Fire into the other elements, and their transmutation back into Fire. Also Democritus who spoke of Fire Atoms, as filling space as the Mind or Soul of the World; and Plato who spoke of a World-Soul, which is composed of Fire Atoms. (Wm. Turner's Hist. of Phil. p. 42; .5; Zeller's Hist. of Phil. p. 53; 149; Plato's Timaeus, 30A; B. D. Alexander's Hist. of Phil., p. 40).

Likewise the doctrine of opposites has been assigned not only to Pythagoras, who spoke of the elements of the unit as odd and even; but also to (a) Heraclitus who spoke of "the

[141]

unity of warring opposites"; (b) Parmenides who spoke of the distinction between Being and Not-Being; (c) Socrates, who spoke of things as being generated from their opposites; and (d) Plato who spoke of Ideas and Noumena as real and perfect; but phenomena as unreal and imperfect. (The Phaedrus of Plato 250; Parmenides 132D; Aristotle Metaphysics I, 6; 987b, 9; Plato Phaedo 70E; Zeller's Hist. of Phil. p. 51; 61, 68; The Timaeus, p. 28).

Furthermore, the doctrines of the Nous (or Mind) or an Intelligent Agency as responsible for creation, has been assigned not only to Anaxagoras, but also to Socrates who spoke of the existence of useful things as the work of an Intelligence: To Plato who spoke of a World-Soul or Mind, as the cause of life and knowledge in the universe and to Democritus, who attached a similar meaning. (Zeller's Hist. of Phil. p. 80; p. 85; Wm. Turner's Hist. of Phil. p. 82; p. 109). The doctrine of the Logos has been assigned to Heraclitus who spoke of Fire as the Logos or creative principle in nature; while the doctrine of the Demiurge, or an Intermediate God who created the world, has been assigned to Plato (Wm. Turner's Hist. of Phil. p. 55, p. 108).

A. *Text of Part II*

The Gods of Order and arrangement in the cosmos are represented by nine gods, in one God-head, called the Ennead. Here Atum (Atom), the source of the Ogdoad, is also retained as the source of the Gods of Order and arrangement. Atum (Atom) names four pairs of parts of his own body, and thus creates eight Gods, who together with himself become nine. These Eight Gods are the created Gods, the first creatures of this world; and Atum (Atom), the Creator God, the Demiurge, of whom Plato spoke. The Gods whom Atum (Atom) projected from his body were

    (i) Shu (Air)
    (ii) Tefnut (Moisture)
    (iii) Geb (Earth) and
    (iv) Nut (Sky);

who are said to have given birth to four other Gods:

  (v) Osiris (the God of omnipotence and omniscience)
  (vi) Isis (wife of Osiris, Female Principle)
  (vii) Seth (the opposite of good)
  (viii) Nephthys (Female Principle in the Unseen World).

(Plutarch: Isis et Osiris, 355A; 364C; 371B; Frankfurt; Intellectual Adventure of Ancient Man, p. 66-67).

B. *The Philosophy of Part II.*

As we read the text of Part II, we find that the Sun God Atum (Atom) who was present in the Chaos was also present at the development of orderly arrangement in the cosmos. At this stage Atum (Atom) assumes the role of creator of all Gods except Ptah, the God of Gods. He next proceeds to accomplish this special type of creation in the following manner: He commands Eight Gods to proceed from His own body according to the names of those eight parts.

The result of this creation presents us with what has been called (a) the "Ennead" or the unity of "nine Gods in one Godhead" '(b) the doctrine of the Demiurge as in Part I, (c) the doctrine of the created Gods and (d) the doctrine of the Unmoved Mover; also (e) the doctrine of opposites and (f) Omnipotence and Omniscience. Of these doctrines, that of the "Ennead" will be dealt with elsewhere, and since the doctrine of the Demiurge has already been treated, together with (c) the created Gods, I shall now discuss the doctrine of the Unmoved Mover, as based upon the same act of creation. According to the Memphite Theology of the Egyptians, Atum created Eight Gods who proceeded from eight parts of His own body. He was seated upon Ptah the Hill and was unmoved. In this act of creation Atum (Atom) became the Unmoved Mover. In spite of the Memphite Theology being the direct source of these doctrines, yet Plato has been given credit for the doctrine of the created Gods; while Aristotle has received credit for that of the "Unmoved Mover". Certainly the world has never been more misled.

Here it must be made quite clear, that the doctrine of a Demiurge in creation includes two other doctrines: that of the created Gods and that of the Unmoved Mover.

It was the function of the Demiurge to create the universe; and in doing so, his first act was the creation of the Gods, who accordingly became the first creatures.

But the manner in which the Demiurge created the Gods was the process of projecting them from His own body.

This method of creation clearly makes the Demiurge the Unmoved Mover.

However the history of Greek philosophy has assigned the authorship of the doctrines of the Demiurge and the created Gods to Plato, and the authorship of the doctrine of the Unmoved Mover to Aristotle.

But this so-called Platonic doctrine is one, made up of three inseparable parts (a) the Demiurge (b) the function of the Demiurge and (c) the method of the function: a unity which contradicts Aristotle's authorship of what is really only an inference from the supposed original doctrine of Plato.

(The Myth of Creation in Plato Timaeus; Wm. Turner; Hist. of Phil., p. 109-110; Zeller's Hist. of Phil. p. 192; Wm. Turner's Hist. of Phil. p. 142).

The doctrine of opposites has already been discussed, however, in Part I of the Memphite Theology. One of the pairs of created Gods, Osiris and Isis was used to represent the male and female principles of nature. In addition to this, Osiris had other qualities attached to Him, which might be understood from the following derivatives (a) osh meaning many, and (b) iri meaning *to do* and also (c) meaning an Eye. Consequently Osiris came to mean not only many eyed or omniscient, but also omnipotent or all powerful. Here again, as in all instances already mentioned, in spite of the fact that the Memphite Theology is the source of Greek philosophy, yet the doctrines of "an Intelligent Cause", a Nous as responsible for the life and conduct of the world, has been assigned to Anaxagoras, Socrates and also Plato, whose World Soul, consisted of fire atoms, like the World Soul of Democritus. (Plato Timaeus 30, 35. Xenophon Memorabilia I, 4, 2; Wm. Turner's Hist. of Phil. 63).

A. *Text of Part III*

In this third part of the Memphite Theology, the Primate of the Gods is represented as Ptah: Thought, Logos and Creative Power, which are exercised over all creatures. He transmits power and spirit to all Gods, and controls the lives of all things, animals and men through His thought and commands. In other words it is in Him that all things live move and have their eternal being.

B. *The Philosophy of Part III*

From Part III we infer the following doctrines:- (a) all things were created by the thought and command of Ptah, the God of Gods. (b) Through the thought and command of Ptah, we all live, move and have our eternal Being. (c) Ptah is Creator and Preserver as has already been pointed out elsewhere; Ptah's powers were transmitted by magical means to Atum who performed the work of creation. (Intellectual Adventures of Man by Frankfort, p. 52-60).

II. **Memphite Theology is the Source of Modern Scientific Knowledge.**
    A. The Ennead and the Nebular Hypothesis.
    B. The identity between the Sun God Atom, and the atom of science.

A. *The Ennead and the Nebular Hypothesis coincide.*

Just as the Memphite Theology is the source of Greek philosophy or primitive science, so it is also the basis of modern scientific belief. The Gods of Order and arrangement in the cosmos are represented by nine Gods in the Godhead, called the Ennead. Atum (Atom), the Sun God, i.e., Fire God, creates eight other Gods, by naming four pairs of parts of his own body, from which they came forth. Here the names of the created Gods were given as Shu and Tefnut (Air and Moisture), Geb and Nut (Earth and Sky); and two other pairs of opposites: Osiris and Isis; and Seth and Nephthys, who are supposed to be the first creatures of this world (Frankfort's Intellectual Adventures of Man, p. 54).

Now if we compare this Egyptian cosmology with the Nebular hypothesis of Laplace, we would find very striking similarities in the two contexts. According to the Nebular hypothesis our present solar system was once a molten gaseous nebula. This nebula rotated at an enormous speed, and as the mass cooled down it also contracted and developed greater speed. The result was a bulging at the equator and a gradual breaking off of gaseous rings, which formed themselves into planets. These planets in turn threw off gaseous rings, which formed themselves into smaller bodies, until at last, the sun was left as the remnant of the original parent Nebula. From this context it is clear that the original parent nebula was fire or the Sun, and that by throwing off parts of itself, it created some planets, which in turn threw off parts of themselves and created others. According to the context of the Memphite Theology, the creator God was the Sun God or fire God Atum (Atom), who named four pairs of parts of his own body, from which Gods came forth.

But Atum (Atom) together with the Eight Created Gods composed the Ennead or Godhead of nine: a very striking similarity with modern science which teaches that there are nine major planets. We may now summarise these similarities:- (a) The creator God in both the Egyptian and Modern Cosmologies is the Sun or Fire. (b) The creator God in both cosmologies creates Gods from parts of Himself. (c) The number of Gods are nine and correspond with the nine major planets. These similarities make it evident that Laplace obtained his hypothesis from the Memphite Theology or other Egyptian sources.

Of course the Memphite Theology, according to Frankfort in his Intellectual Adventure of Ancient Man, p. 54 does not mention the creation of planets. Nevertheless, since it was the method of the Egyptian to conceal the truth by the use of myths, parables magical principles (primitive scientific method), number philosophy and hieroglyphics, we can easily see what methods might be involved before we could arrive at a better translation of the Memphite Theology.

At any rate, the entire setting of the Memphite Theology is astronomical, and what could be more natural, than to expect an astronomical interpretation? It seems well within reason, to regard the Ennead as the heliocentric system of history. Atom the sun God, creating eight other Gods or planets from his own body, as the Unmoved Mover a teaching which has been falsely attributed to Aristotle.

B. *The identity between the Egyptian Sun God Atum (Atom) and the atom of Modern Science*:

There are two things which I desire to point out in connexion with the relationship between Atum (Atom) the Egyptian Sun God and the atom of modern science. These things are (i) the similarity of attributes and (ii) the similarity of names. (i) The Egyptian God Atum (Atom) means self-created; everything and nothing; a combination of positive and negative principles:- all-inclusiveness and emptiness; a Demiurge, possessing creative powers; the Creator Sun. (p. 53, Frankfort's Intellectual Adventure of Ancient Man; p. 182, Frankfort's Kingship and the Gods).

Atum (Atom) also means "the all and the not yet Being"; (p. 168 Frankfort's Kingship of the Gods). As a God Atum (Atom) represents the principles of opposites. The atom, as the substratum of matter, according to Greek philosophy, is defined by Democritus as "movement of that which is" (*To on*) within "that which is not" (το *mē on*). It therefore represents the principle of opposites, and shows the identity between the Egyptian Sun God and the substratum of matter. Furthermore, the atom is defined as "the full and void; being and not-being (Zeller's Hist. of Phil., p. 38) and these definitions coincide with the everything and nothing, and the "all-inclusiveness" and emptiness of the Egyptian Sun God.

(ii) *The similarity of names shared by the Egyptian Sun God and the atom of science*:

Now, with reference to the similarity of these two names, the first thing we should bear in mind is the fact that they both possess identical attributes, as has been already pointed out in section i; and consequently we are compelled to conclude that the atom of science is the identical name of the Egyptian Sun God: the most ancient of Gods except Ptah, who was present with Atom at creation. The second thing we should bear in mind is the fact that the name of the God Atom (sometimes spelt Atum) belongs to the cosmology of the Memphite Theology, whose date goes back to 4000 B. C. when the Greeks were not even known. Consequently we are compelled to conclude that the Greeks obtained both the original name and the attributes of the Sun God Atom from the Egyptians.

Furthermore, the Greeks were unacquainted with the Egyptian language, during the period of the so-called Greek philosophy, dating from the sixth century B. C. and as a consequence transliterated Egyptian words into Greek without regard to their coptic derivatives. The following Homeric stories verify the practice of the Greeks in the transliteration of Egyptian words and the plagiarism of their legends. (a) According to Homer, Proteus was a Maritime Divinity feeding his phocae on the coast of Egypt. He was endowed with the gift of prophecy which was exercised only upon compulsion. Proteus, however was an Egyptian Pharaoh who succeeded to the throne on the death of Pheron, the son of Sesostris. Proteus was also worshipped at Memphis. The Greeks did not only transliterate the name of this Egyptian King, but also plagiarized on the legend. (Herodotus II, 112).

(b) Likewise the story of Io the Argive Princess, who was changed into a heifer, and after long wanderings, reached

Egypt, where she gave birth to a God, and where she herself was worshipped as the Goddess Isis, points clearly to the introduction of the worship of Isis or Athor, under the symbol of the heifer, at an early period into Argos. Here it must be pointed out that Io is the Coptic name for Moon, and the same word was preserved as the dialect of Argos, without any affinity with any Greek root. It was a habit of the Greeks to Hellenize Egyptian words by transliterating them and adding them to the Greek vocabulary.

(c) This practice of borrowing words from nearby nations continued until New Testament times. In Acts of Apostles of the Greek Testament, Chapter 13th and verse 1, the word Niger (i.e., black man) in the name Simeon the Negro is a Roman or Latin word (niger, nigra, nigrum) meaning black. Simeon, of course, was an Egyptian Professor attached to the Church at Rome.

The atom of science is really the name of the Egyptian Sun God that has come down to modern times, through the so-called Greek philosophy, and carries identical attributes, with the Sun God. (Diodorus I, 29; John Kendrick's Ancient Egypt, vol. II 5-52; Eust. ad Dionys: Perieg: V).

N. B.

It must be remembered that what we erroneously call Greek philosophy, was the beginning of science or the investigation of nature; and consequently we cannot separate modern science from Greek philosophy.

III. Memphite Theology Opens Great Possibilities for Modern Scientific Research.

A. *Greek Concept of the Atom; erroneous.*

The Greeks derived the meaning of the atom from (i) (*alpha*) i.e. a negative prefix meaning not; and (ii) (*temnein*) i.e. the present infinitive active of (*temno*) to cut. The two derivatives together meaning "that which cannot be cut". For centuries the world has been misled by this misconception of the Greeks: a fact which no doubt, had impeded the progress of atomic research by Western scholars, who had believed in the so-called Greek origin of philosophy or primitive science.

Today, however, the Greek conception of the atom is no longer tenable, since modern science has successfully split the atom.

B. *Great scientific secrets in the Memphite Theology, yet to be discovered.*

I believe that the time has come, within which man will be able to unlock most of the secrets of nature hitherto hidden and unknown. I have shown that the Nebular Hypothesis of modern times coincides with the teachings of the Memphite Theology, in which the Sun God Atom is said to have created eight other Gods, which together with himself constitute the Ennead of the Egyptians, which correspond to the nine major planets of modern scientific teaching.

We also know that out of Cosmic Chaos there arose from the primeval waters a pair of Gods i.e. the Primeval Hill and Atom the Sun God, and that through the contact of Atom with the Hill, He received power to create the other eight major planets. This seems to imply that

(i) Atomic energy originates from water and earth, since water H_2O, and uranium, an indispensable ingredient in atomic energy, is found in the bowels of the earth. Note that both Atom and the Hill came out of the primeval Waters.

(ii) Four pairs of Gods, representing positive and negative principles still remain in water, in the form of male and female frogs and snakes, and constitute four fifths of the secrets of creation, which man has yet to fathom.

(iii) Successful scientific research in the principles and secrets of nature lies in the study of the Memphite Theology, whose symbology requires the key of magical principles for its interpretation. With this approach our men of science should be able to unlock the doors of the secrets of nature and become the custodians of unlimited knowledge.

This is the legacy of the African Continent to the nations of the world. She has laid the cultural foundations of modern progress and therefore she and her people deserve the honour and praise which for centuries have been falsely given to the Greeks. And likewise, it is the purpose of this book to make this revelation the beginning of a universal reformation in race relations, which I believe would be the beginning of the solution of the problem of universal unrest.

PART II

CHAPTER IX:

Social Reformation through the New Philosophy of African Redemption.

Now that it has been shown that philosophy, and the arts and sciences were bequeathed to civilization by the people of No.th Africa and not by the people of Greece; the pendulum of praise and honour is due to shift from the people of Greece to the people of the African continent who are the rightful heirs of such praise and honour.

This is going to mean a tremendous change in world opinion, and attitude, for all people and races who accept the new philosophy of African redemption, ie the truth that the Greeks were not the authors of Greek philosophy; but the people of North Africa; would change their opinion from one of disrespect to one of respect for the Black people throughout the world and treat them accordingly.

It is also going to mean a most important change in the mentality of the Black people: a change from an inferiority complex, to the realization and consciousness of their equality with all the other great peoples of the world, who have built great civilizations. With this change in the mentality of the Black and White people, great changes are also expected in their respective attitudes towards each other, and in society as a whole.

In the drama of Greek philosophy there are three actors, who have played distinct parts, namely Alexander the Great, who by an act of agression invaded Egypt in 333 B. C., and ransacked and looted the Royal Library at Alexandria and together with his companions carried off a booty of scientific, philosophic and religious books. Egypt was then stolen and annexed as a portion of Alexander's empire; but the invasion plan included far more than mere territorial expansion; for it prepared the way and made it possible for the capture of the culture of the African Continent. This brings us to the second actor, that is the School of Aristotle whose students moved from Athens to Egypt and converted the royal library, first into a research centre, and secondly into a University and thirdly compiled that vast body of scientific knowledge which they had gained from research, together with the oral instructions which Greek students had received from the Egyptian priests, into what they have called the history of Greek Philosophy.

In this way, the Greeks stole the Legacy of the African Continent and called it their own. And as has already been pointed out, the result of this dishonesty has been the creation of an erroneous world opinion; that the African continent has made no contribution to civilization, because her people are backward and low in intelligence and culture.

This erroneous opinion about the Black people has seriously injured them through the centuries up to modern times in which it appears to have reached a climax in the history of human relations. And now we come to the third actor, and that is Ancient Rome, who through the edicts of her Emperors Theodosius in the 4th century A. D. and Justinian in the 6th century A. D. abolished the Mysteries of the African Continent; that is the ancient culture system of the world. The higher metaphysical doctrines of those Mysteries could not be comprehended; the spiritual powers of the priests were unsurpassed; the magic of the rites and ceremonies filled the people with awe; Egypt was the holy land of the ancient world and the Mysteries were the one, ancient and holy Catholic religion, whose power was supreme. This lofty culture system of the Black people filled Rome with envy, and consequently she legalized Christianity which she had persecuted for five long centuries, and set it up as a state religion and as a rival of Mysteries, its own mother. This is why the Mysteries have been despised; this is why other ancient religions of the Black

[154]

people are despised; because they are all offspring of the African Mysteries, which have never been clearly understood by Europeans, and consequently have provoked their prejudice and condemnation. In keeping with the plan of Emperors Theodosius and Justinian to exterminate and forever suppress the culture system of the African continents the Christian church established its missionary enterprise to fight against what it has called paganism. Consequently missionaries and educators have gone to the mission field with a superiority complex, born of miseducation and disrespect: a prejudice which has made it impossible for them to accomplish the blessings which missionary enterprise might otherwise have accomplished. For this reason Missionary enterprise has been responsible for a positive injury against the African people, which consists of the perpetual caricature of African culture in literature and exhibitions which provoke laughter and disrespect. This then is only a brief summary of the parts played by the persons of the drama of Greek philosophy and the resultant effects upon the Black people. This drama might be called the Causa Causarum of the social plight of the peoples of African descent, because it has made the White and Black races not only common victims of a false racial tradition about the African Continent but also partners in the solution of the problem of racial reformation.

I believe that a reformation of this kind is possible, if the best minds of both racial groups co-operate in its accomplishment. Both groups have been the common victims of miseducation arising from a false tradition about the African Continent and it has caused them to develop attitudes according to their common belief: The White people, a superiority complex; and the Black people, the corresponding inferiority complex; and if we are to accomplish a reformation in race relations it is obvious that both racial groups must combine their efforts in the abandonment and destruction of that mentality which has plunged the Black people into their social plight.

This I suggest should be done by a world wide dissemina-

[155]

tion of the truth, through a system of re-education, in order
to stimulate and encourage a change in the attitude of races
toward each other In combining their efforts, both races
must not only preach and teach the truth that the Mystery
system of the African Continent gave the world philosophy
and religion, and the arts and sciences, but they must see to
it that all false praise of the Greeks be removed from the
textbooks of our schools and colleges: for this is the practice
that has blind-folded the world, and has laid the foundations
for the deplorable race relations of the modern world. (a)
The name of Pythagoras, for instance, should be deleted from
our mathematical textbooks: in Geometry, where the theorem
of the square on the hypotenuse of a right angled triangle
is called the Pythagorean theorem, because this is not true.
(b) we must point out to the world the deception in attaching the authorship of Socrates to the precept 'man know thyself'; and in attaching the authorship of Plato to the four cardinal virtues; since Socrates obtained the self-knowledge precept from the Egyptian temples where it was used as an inscription; and Plato reduced the ten virtues of the North
African Mystery system to four (c) we must also prove to
the world that the doctrines of the so-called Greek philosophers originated from the ancient Mystery System of North
Africa.

This proof has been set forth in chapters five to eight of
'Stolen Legacy,' and in order to carry out our world-wide cru-
sade we must recommend 'Stolen Legacy,' for adoption and
study in the schools and colleges of both racial groups and in
our fraternities, sororities and inter-racial groups, in order
that young and old of our present generation might all get to
know the truth and be able to pass it on to future generations.

This I believe would be a very helpful method by which
this process of re-education would become universal and effective in the creation of a much needed racial reformation.
The White people of our modern age cannot be regarded as
wholly responsible for social conditions which are the result

of false racial tradition. It is this that makes race relations a challenge to the best minds of both racial groups to combine their efforts in its solution.

But our disturbed race relations have also another cause. This I would say is both supplementary and intensive; for the false tradition about the backwardness of the African Continent, created by Alexander the Great and Aristotle's School has been dramatized by missionary literature and exhibitions, as the will of Roman Emperors and as a source of laughter and disrespect. There is no doubt that this policy has created bitterness and dissatisfaction in the minds of ˪atives, who have been compelled to question the sincerity of the missionary. In the meantime missionary enterprise gains the sympathy and support of a miseducated world, in order to carry on its programme.

What can we do to eradicate this second and more subtle evil: the dramatization of a false tradition so as to make it appear as true? I suggest that since the missionary dramatizes false tradition because he himself also believes it, we should combine our efforts, first of all in re-educating him so that he might know the truth and change his superiority complex which is responsible for his mistaken policy. His re-education should not only consist of a thorough study of the ideas and arguments contained in my book 'Stolen Legacy'; but he must also be given special training in the language, customs and ideals of Africans, in order to make him cultivate an attitude of respect for the culture of the African Continent, seemingly the oldest specimen to have been developed by mankind; because that continent is the birth place and the cradle of the Ancient Mysteries. With a world enlightened as to the real truth about the place of the African Continent in the history of civilization, false tradition and belief should cease to be effective, disrespect and prejudice should tend to disappear, and race relations should tend to be normal and peaceful. This brings us to the final problem, the problem of African redemption. The aims of 'Stolen Legacy' are not only to stimulate a reformation in race relations and scientific research; but also to cultivate race pride in the Black people themselves and to offer them a New Philosophy of African Redemption as the Modus Operandi of achieving racial reformation.

This New Philosophy of Redemption consists of a simple proposition as follows:

'The Greeks were not the authors of Greek philosophy, but the Black people of North Africa, The Egyptians.'

Now, in order to explain the value of this proposition, three questions must be asked and answered.

(a) *As a simple proposition, what is its significance?*

Its significance lies in the fact that it is a statement of an important truth, which is the exposure of Greek dishonesty.

(b) *Why is this proposition called a philosophy?*

A philosophy is an accepted belief, and this proposition is a philosophy because it is offered as a belief, worthy of acceptance.

(c) *What is a philosophy of redemption?*

A philosophy of redemption is not merely an accepted belief; but a belief that is also lived in order to enjoy the benefits of its teaching.

This proposition will become a philosophy of redemption to all Black people, when they accept it as a belief and live up to it. This brings us to our final question and that is, *how to live up to this philosophy of redemption? In other words, how shall the Black people work out their own salvation?*

From the outset my readers and co-workers in the solution of a common problem, must be reminded that our philosophy of redemption is a psychological process, involving a change in belief or mentality to be followed by a corresponding change in behaviour. *It really signifies a mental emancipation, in which the Black people will be liberated from the chain of traditional falsehood,* which for centuries has incarcerated them in the prison of inferiority complex and world humiliation and insult. This mental emancipation or redemption, it must be remembered, has two functions. It is general, when, on the one hand, the phenomenon of our unwholesome race relations is regarded as a general problem needing a general emancipation of both races in order to effect a solution. In this general sense emancipation transcends the limitations and boundaries of race, and therefore includes the whole world, White and Black people, since we are all victims of the same chain of the traditional falsehood, that has incarcerated the modern world. On the other hand, emancipation or redemption is specific, when we refer to the effects of the phenomenon of unwholesome race relations upon the Black people. It is freedom from such conditions that constitutes the specific function of emancipation or redemption.

We digressed somewhat in order to explain the terms philosphy and philosophy of redemption, believing it to be necessary before proceeding to answer the next question: how to live up to this New Philosophy of Redemption? How must it be worked out?

Being liberated from inferiority complex by their New Philosophy of Redemption, which is destined to destroy the chain of false tradition which has incarcerated them, the Black people must face and interpret the world according to their new vision and philosophy. Throughout the centuries up to our modern times, world conditions have been influenced by two phenomena which have affected human relations.

(i) The giving of false praise to the Greeks: a custom which appears to be an educational policy conducted by educational institutions. This has led to the false worship of Socrates, Plato, and Aristotle, as intellectual gods in all the leading universities of the world, and in support of this intellectual worship, these institutions have also organized what are known as Greek lettered fraternities and sororities, as the symbols of the superiority of Greek intellect and culture.

(ii) The second phenomenon is Missionary enterprise whereby the Black people's culture has been caricatured in literature and exhibitions, in such specimens as provoke disrespect and laughter. Never let us forget that the Roman Emperors Theodosius and Justinian were responsible for the abolition of the Egyptian Mysteries that is the culture system of the Black people, and also for the establishment of Christianity for its perpetual suppression.

Likewise, never let us forget when we are reviewing this bit of history that the Greeks called the Egyptians Hoi Aiguptoi which meant Black people.

In living up to their New Philosophy of Redemption, the life of the Black people will have to be one of counteraction against these two sets of conditions. In the first place the Black people must adopt a negative attitude towards this type of phenomena, because they have become fully aware that these phenomena are the result of a false tradition, and therefore also partake of the nature of falsehood and insincerity.

In this negative attitude the Black people of the world must shun the false tradition and must teach the truth, which is their New Philosophy of Redemption. This must be done in the home to young children; in the colleges and schools to students; from the pulpits and platforms to audiences; and in the fraternities and sororities to young men and women. This New Philosophy of Redemption, being a revelation of truth in the history of Black people's civilization must become a necessary portion of their education, and must be taught for generations and centuries to come; in order to fill them with inspiration and pride and liberate them from mental servitude.

In the second place, in this negative attitude the Black people must demonstrate their disbelief in the false worship of Greek intellect. This should be done in the following three ways:—

(i) They must discontinue the practice of quoting Socrates, Plato and Aristotle in their speeches as intellectual models; because we know that their philosophy was stolen (ii) They must relinquish membership from all Greek lettered fraternities and sororities and (iii) They must abolish all Greek lettered fraternities and sororities from all colored colleges because they have been a source of the promotion of inferiority complex and of educating the Black people against themselves. We come now to the counteraction of the second set of phenomena, the missionary activities in defamatory literature and exhibitions which provoke disrespect for and laughter at the Black people.

Just as in the first set of phenomena, so is it in the second, the Black people must adopt a negative attitude in their attempt to live up to their philosophy of redemption. Of course, they are perfectly well aware that the activities of missionaries are the result of their own miseducation through the medium of a false tradition about Black people; but since their problem is also one of emancipation from certain social evils, the Black people feel that they are entitled to a change in Missionary policy. For these reasons I suggest that the negative attitude of the Black people should consist first of a boycott of missionary literature and exhibitions, and secondly, of a perpetual protest against these forms of missionary policy, until a change is brought about. For as long as Missionary enterprise maintains its policy of militancy against African culture, the Black people will be disrespected. This is the least that the Black people are entitled to: respectful treatment, because they are the representatives of the oldest civilization in the world, from which all other cultures have borrowed. I have frequently seen in the parish magazines of some European churches, pictures of the following description:— An African Chief, dressed in a new silk hat, a long shirt, but no trousers, a frock coat and barefeet; probably to provide amusement for the parishioners and to excite their pity. This is what the Black people must protest against and this is how they must live up to their philosophy of redemption and work it out.

In conclusion, let us remember that the unfortunate position of the modern church in being associated with the drama of Greek philosophy is excusable; because her missionary function has been due to the erroneous mandates and edicts of secular Princes and Emperors, who ruled the church, when it was only

[161]

a department of state. This bit of ecclesiastical history should be well known to the early branches of the Christian church and consequently, they are the ones whom our enlightened age expects to initiate a change in missionary policy, which would free themselves from the error and superstition of human relations.

This lead of the various branches of Catholicism should be followed by Protestantism, so that the entire church of Christ on earth should be united in this racial reformation, and carry to the mission field a practical gospel of happiness; that is happiness that must begin while we are here on earth; a gospel that is interested in the total welfare of the people. A gospel which ignores the social and economic rights of natives and emphasizes only happiness in an unknown world is onesided, misleading, and contrary to Christian tenets and practice. It was early Christianity that established a diaconate for the express purpose of solving the economic problems of its adherents; so that they might begin in their earthly life to experience what happiness realy meant.

It is evident that the benefits of religion are intended to be coextensive with human needs and unless the Christian religion changes its missionary policy with respect to the Culture of the Black people, it would be difficult for them to obtain complete emancipation from the social injuries created by Ancient Rome.

APPENDIX

THE PURPOSE of this appendix is to present a brief analysis and summary of the arguments, conclusions and inferences which relate to the subject matter which has already been treated. It is also hoped that it will serve the secondary purpose of simplification.

ARGUMENT I. *Greek philosophy was stolen Egyptian philosophy.*

Because history tells us that (i) The teachings of the Egyptian Mystery System travelled from Egypt to the island Samos, and from Samos to Croton and Elea in Italy, and lastly from Italy to Athens in Greece through the medium of Pythagoras and the Eleatic and late Ionic philosophers. Accordingly, Egypt was the true source of the Mystery teachings and therefore any claim to such origin by the ancient Greeks is not only erroneous but must have been based upon dishonest motives.

(ii) History also represents the early life and education of Greek philosophers as a blank and their chronology as a matter of speculation. Consequently it has given the world the opinion that the Greek philosophers, with the exception of the three Athenians, might never have existed and might never have taught the doctrines alleged to them. In other words History represents the Pre-Socratic philosophers as questionable in existence and under those circumstances they could neither produce philosophy nor claim its authorship, except by questionable and dishonest methods.

(iii) The compilation of Greek philosophy appears to have been the idea of Aristotle, but the work of the alumni of his school. The movement was unauthorized by the Greek Government which always hated and persecuted philosophy, because it was Egyptian and foreign. The organization, control and operation of the Mysteries gave the Egyptians the right of ownership to philosophy, and therefore any claims by the ancient Greeks to philosophy must be considered as illegal and dishonest.

ARGUMENT II. *So-called Greek philosophy was alien to the Greeks.*

Because (i) the period of Greek philosophy (Thales to Aristotle) was a period of internal wars among the city states themselves and external wars with their common enemy, the Persians. The Greeks were victims of perpetual internal strife and perpetual fear of annihi-

[163]

lation by their common enemy. They had no time which they could devote to the study of nature, for this required the riches and wealth of the leisure classes: but they were too poor to engage in such a pursuit. This is one of the reasons why the Greek philosophers were so few and why the Greeks were unacquainted with philosophy.

(ii) The Greeks did not possess the native ability essential to the development of philosophy. The death of Aristotle, who had inherited a vast quantity of books from the library of Alexandria through his friendship with Alexander the Great, was also followed by the death of Greek philosophy which soon degenerated into a system of borrowed ideas known as eclecticism. This system contained nothing new in spite of the great treasure of knowledge which they had obtained through Alexander's friendship with Aristotle and his conquest of Egypt.

(iii) The Greeks rejected and persecuted philosophy owing to the fact that it came from an outside and foreign source and contained strange ideas with which they were unacquainted. This prejudice led to the policy of persecution. Hence Anaxagoras was indicted and escaped from prison and fled to Ionia in exile. Socrates was executed; Plato fled to Megara to the rescue of Euclid; and Aristotle was indicted and escaped into exile. This policy of the Greeks would be meaningless, if it did not indicate that philosophy was alien to Greek mentality.

ARGUMENT III. *Greek philosophy was the offspring of the Egyptian Mystery System.*

Because complete identity had been found to exist between the Egyptian Mystery System and Greek philosophy with the only exception of age in relation of parent to child. The Egyptian Mystery System antedated that of Greece by many thousands of years. The following are the circumstances and conditions of identity:—

(i) Complete agreement between the Egyptian theory of salvation and the purpose of Greek philosophy, i. e., to make man become God-like by virtue and educational disciplines.

(ii) Complete agreement of the conditions of initiation into both systems, i. e., preparation (in gradual stages of virtue) before every initiation.

(iii) Complete agreement in tenets and practice.

(iv) History tells us that the remains of the Ancient Grand Temple of Luxor have been traced to the banks of the Nile in the ancient city of Thebes, a short distance from Danderah, now called upper Egypt. It also tells us that this Grand Temple was constructed by Pharaoh Amenothis III who began it, and Rameses II who completed it. At the time of Greek philosophy, the Mystery System of Egypt was the only such system in the ancient world, and therefore its Grand Lodge was the only such Grand Lodge in existence. It was the seat of government, having organized the ancient world into a universal or catholic brotherhood with jurisdiction over all minor lodges and schools wherever they were. And whether we call it the Mysteries or Greek philosophy or Free Masonry, the system was one and all branches came out of that one and were subordinate to it.

(v) The identity between the Egyptian Mysteries and Greek philosophy is also established by the fact that when the Roman Emperors Theodosius and Justinian issued their edicts closing down the Egyptian Mysteries, the effect was the same upon the philosophical schools in Greece, for they had to be closed. Things which are affected equally by the same cause are themselves equal.

ARGUMENT IV. *The Egyptians educated the Greeks.*

Because History supports the following facts:—

(i) *The effects of the Persian conquest upon Egypt*
(a) Removed immigration restrictions against the Greeks.

(b) Opened up Egypt to Greek research and (c) encouraged students from Ionia and elsewhere to visit Egypt for the purpose of their education.

(ii) *The effects of the conquest of Alexander the Great upon Egypt*
(a) It was the custom of ancient armies when invading countries to search for treasures in libraries and temples. Accordingly it is believed that Alexander and his friends who accompanied him ransacked the Library of Alexandria and other libraries and helped themselves with books. It is also believed that this was how Aristotle got the vast quantity of books alleged to his authorship and how he acquired exaggerated fame.

(b) The Library of Alexandria was taken over by the Alumni of Aristotle's school and converted into a research centre and University, for the education of the Greeks who were compelled to use Egyptian Professors, on account of linguistic difficulties and other reasons.

(c) Apart from the looting of libraries and the conversion of the Library of Alexandria into a University for their education, the Greeks had another way of adopting the culture of the Egyptians. The Ptolemies used to commandeer useful information from the Egyptian High Priests, and we are told that Ptolemy I Soter commanded the High Priest Manetho to write a history of religion and philosophy of the Egyptians and this was done and the volumes became the chief text books in the University of Alexandria.

STOLEN LEGACY

(iii) *The Egyptians were the first to civilize the Greeks*

History tells us that the Greeks received the influence of civilization from three sources: colonizers first from Egypt, colonizers secondly from Phoenicia and colonizers thirdly from Thrace. It also tells us that these colonies were under the government of wise men who subdued the ferocity of the ignorant populace, not only by means of civil institutions, but also by the strong chain of religion and the fear of the Gods. Those colonizers were Cecrops from Egypt, Cadmus from Phoenicia and Orpheus from Thrace.

ARGUMENT V. *The doctrines of Greek philosophers are the doctrines of the Egyptian Mystery System.*

The proof of this proposition is really one of the main purposes of this book and hence chapters five and six have been devoted to this purpose. The Egyptian teachings were expressed in symbols of various types and therefore their origin can be established by reference to the particular symbol in question. In these chapters therefore mention has been made not only of the names of Greek philosophers and the doctrines which have been ascribed to them; but also the necessary references to the particular types of symbology, in proof of their Egyptian origin. These have been given in the Summary of Conclusions as follow:—

1. *The early Ionic philosophers* have been credited with the doctrines that (a) all things originated from water (b) all things originated from the boundless or primitive chaos and (c) all things originated from air. But these doctrines could not have been those of the Ionic philosophers; since we find the same ideas expressed in the first chapter of Genesis, where we are told that at the beginning the world was in a state of chaos, without form and void (boundless); and how the spirit of God (air) moved upon the waters and separated them from dry land and earth from sky; and how step by step, living things came out of the waters and how finally, through the breath of life (air) man came into existence. Genesis is the first book of the Pentateuch whose date has been placed to the Eighth Century B. C.: a time when the early Ionic philosophers did not even exist and who therefore could not have been the authors of these doctrines. Similarly, the authorship of Genesis has been ascribed to Moses, who Philo tells us was an Egyptian Priest, a Hierogrammat, and learned in all the wisdom of the Egyptians. But the age in which Moses lived must be associated with the Exodus of the Israelites which he conducted in the 21st Egyptian Dynasty: 1100 B. C. in the reign of Bocchoris. But the creation story of Genesis coincides with the crea-

[166]

tion story of the Memphite Theology of the Egyptians, which takes us back to between 4 and 5 thousand B. C. This means that the doctrines of the early Ionians arose neither at their time (the fifth century B. C.), nor at the time of Pentateuch (the eighth century B. C.), nor yet at the time of Moses (the eleventh century B. C.), but at the time of the Memphite Theology (betwen 4 and 5 thousand B. C.) and therefore definitely point to Egyptian origin.

2. *The Eleatic philosophers* have been named as (i) Zenophanes who was a satirist (ii) Zeno whose treatment of space and time led to a reductio ad absurdum and (iii) Parmenides who alone deserves notice. He has been credited with the definitions of Being and non-Being, which he expressed as 'that which is' and 'that which is not'. In other words, nature or reality consists of two properties, i. e., a positive and a negative. But Parmenides introduced no new doctrine, when he defined the principle of opposites. This principle was used by Pythagoras in his theory of numbers; by Socrates in his proof of the immortality of the Soul; by Plato in his Theory of Ideas and the distinction between phenomena and noumena; and by Aristotle in his definition of the attributes of Being. In all these instances it has been shown that the doctrine of opposites originated from the Egyptian Mystery System, in connection with which Gods were represented as male and female, and temples carried double pillars in front of them to indicate positive and negative principles of nature.

3. *The late Ionic philosophers* have been named as (i) Heracleitus who taught that the world was produced by fire, through a process of transmutation; and that since all things originate from Fire, then Fire is the Logos.

(ii) Anaxagoras, who taught that Mind or Nous is the source of life in the Universe and

(iii) Democritus, who taught that atoms underlie all material things; that life and death are merely changes brought about by variation in the mixture of atoms, which do not die because they are immortal. Now, taking these doctrines in the order in which they come, their Egyptian origin has been fully established.

(a) The doctrine of Fire has been traced to the Egyptians, whose Mystery System was a Fire Philosophy and who worshipped the God of Fire in their pyramids. The word pyramid is a Greek word, whose derivative pyr means fire. This doctrine takes us back to the pyramid age in Egypt 33 hundred B. C. when, of course, the Greeks were unknown.

(b) It must be noted that the doctrine of the Logos has been identified by Heracleitus with the doctrine of Fire. This is as it should be, because (c) in the doctrine of the created Gods which has been ascribed to Plato, Atom the Sun God or Fire performs the function of Demiurge in creating the Gods.

(d) Similarly in the doctrine of the Unmoved Mover ascribed to Aristotle, the Fire God Atom while unmoved and sitting upon the Primeval Hill, creates the Gods by commanding them to proceed from various parts of His own body. In this way Atom also became the Unmoved Mover. This makes it clear that the Logos of Heracleitus is identical with the Demiurge of Plato and the Unmoved Mover of Aristotle. The function of Atom as Demiurge and the method of His creation are found in the Memphite Theology of the Egyptians. Here I would like to suggest that students who are interested in tracing the influence of Egyptian philosophy upon Christian thought, should read this portion of my book together with the first chapter of St. John's gospel. The problem of permanence and change is also traced in the Creation story of the Memphite Theology in which eternal matter is represented by chaos, and change by the gradual formation of order.

(e) The doctrine of Mind or Nous, has been ascribed not only to Anaxagoras, but also to Democritus who spoke of it as being composed of fire atoms distributed throughout the universe and Socrates who has been credited with the teleological premise: that whatsoever exists for a useful purpose is the work of an Intelligence. This doctrine has been traced to the Egyptian Mystery System, in which the God Osiris was represented by an Open Eye; signifying not only omniscience, but also omnipotence. All Masonic lodges carry this symbol with the same meaning today.

(f) The doctrine of the atom has been ascribed to Democritus, who does not define but describes its properties. It is the basis of life; it is immortal and does not die; and when many of them are mixed in certain ways the result is a radical change. These properties coincide with the properties of Atom the Sun God and the Demiurge in creation, who created other Gods from various parts of himself. He was the basis of life and giver of life. But Atom the Sun God occurs in the creation story of the Memphite Theology and shows the Egyptian origin of the atom.

4. *The system of Pythagoras* seems to have been so comprehensive that nearly all subsequent philosophers have copied ideas from his teachings. Interpreting nature in the form of mathematics, Pythagoras is credited with teaching the following doctrines:—

(a) *The properties of Number* include opposite elements: odd and even, finite and infinite, and positive and negative. This principle of opposites was copied by and used in the teachings of Heracleitus, Parmenidies, Democritus, Socrates, Plato and Aristotle.

(b) *The doctrine of Harmony*, defined as the union of opposites. This idea was copied by and used in the teachings of Heracleitus, Socrates, Plato and Aristotle.

(c) *Fire (central and peripheral)* was taught to be the basis of creation. This doctrine was also used by and in the teachings of Heracleitus, Anaxagoras, Democritus, Socrates and Plato.

(d) *The immortality of the soul and The Summum Bonum.* This was taught by Pythagoras in the form of a transmigration of the soul. It was also taught by Socrates as the purpose of philosophy through which, the soul feeding upon the truth congenial to its divine nature, was enabled to escape the wheel of rebirth and to attain the final consummation of unity with God. All the doctrines of Pythagoras have been shown to originate from the Egyptian Mystery System. Number possesses opposite elements and the principle of opposites belongs to the Egyptian Mystery System in which it was represented by male and female Gods. Harmony being a blending of opposites, needs no further reference, and Fire likewise takes us back to the Egyptian Mystery System which was a Fire Philosophy and its Initiates Fire worshippers. Finally, the purpose of philosophy was the salvation of the soul. This was accomplished by methods of purification offered by the Egyptian Mysteries, which lifted man from the mortal to the immortal level. This was the Summum Bonum, The Greatest Good.

5. *Socrates (A) His life and (B) His doctrines (C) His indictment, condemnation and death (D) His farewell conversations.*

A. *In his life* he voluntarily adopted secrecy and poverty, in order that he might avoid the temptation of riches and be enabled to cultivate the virtues required by the Mysteries.

B. *All his doctrines* likewise associate him with the Egyptian Mysteries.

(i) His doctrine of the Mind or Nous as Intelligence which underlies creation, was represented in Egyptian temples, just as in modern Masonic temples, by the "Open Eye of Osiris", indicating omniscience and omnipotence.

(ii) His doctrine of self knowledge: "Man know thyself" was copied directly or indirectly from among the inscriptions which appeared on the outside of the Mystery temples in Egypt.

(iii) His doctrines of Opposites and Harmony were a testimony of the custom of the Mysteries to demonstrate the principle of opposites in nature by pairs of male and female Gods and also by double pillars in front of temples.

(iv) His doctrines of Immortality, Salvation of the Soul and The Summum Bonum were a summary of the theory of salvation as was taught by the Mysteries. Socrates himself explained it. The purpose of philosophy was the salvation of the soul by a process of purification which lifted man from the mortal level and raised him to the immortal. This was an attainment, this was the Summum Bonum or Greatest Good.

C. His indictment, condemnation and death are circumstances which also show his association with the Mysteries. He was indicted for the introduction of foreign Gods and the corruption of Athenian Youth and was condemned and put to death. The foreign Gods were the Gods of the Mysteries and his submission to martyrdom was due on the one hand to the prejudice of the Athenian authorities, while on the other hand, to his virtue of courage, required by the Mysteries.

D. His farewell conversations also show his membership with the great Egyptian Order. There are two accounts of these conversations: one by Crito and the other by Phaedo. Crito describes the brotherly behaviour of a band of faithful friends and Neophytes who visited him daily while he was in prison awaiting his execution. The purpose of these visits was to secure the escape of a brother; but their efforts were in vain, for he refused to yield to their entreaties. Phaedo mentions that the theme of the other conversation was the immortality of the soul in which Socrates endeavoured to give them some proofs by his application of the principles of opposites. We are also told that towards the end of the conversations, and just before he drank the poison, Socrates requested Crito to pay for him a certain debt which he owed. These conversations reveal the following facts:—

(a) The brotherly love of the visiting Neophytes in their attempt to secure the escape of their brother Socrates.

(b) A final class was conducted by Socrates on the doctrine of immortality: the central doctrine of the Egyptian Mysteries and

(c) A final request of Socrates to have a debt paid for him and

(d) These conversations constitute the earliest specimen of Masonic literature. All four of which facts point to membership in the Egyptian Mystery System. It was a Universal Brotherhood and required the cultivation of brotherly love. Its central teaching was the immortality of the soul, and it also required all Initiates to practice the virtues of justice and honesty and therefore to pay their debts.

E. It is believed that Socrates did not commit his teachings to writings. This was also in obedience to the secrecy of the Mysteries.

6. *Plato*

(A) His early life and education as in the case of all other philosophers are unknown to history, which represents him as fleeing from Athens after the death of Socrates and after twelve years during which time he visited Euclid at Megara, the Pythagoreans in Italy, Dionysius in Sicily and the Mystery System in Egypt, he returned to Athens and opened an Academy, where he taught for 20 years.

(B) His doctrines which are scattered over a wide area of literature consisting of 36 dialogues are disputed by modern scholarship. The pupils of Socrates especially Plato are supposed to have published his teachings, and it is not known how much of this vast literature belongs to Plato and how much to Socrates. The doctrines of Plato have all been traced to Egyptian origin.

(i) The Theory of Ideas, which he illustrated by reference to the phenomena of nature, is a distinction between the Ideas or noumena and their copies the phenomena; and between the real and unreal, by the application of the principle of opposites, which was manifested by the Egyptian Mystery System by male and female Gods and pairs of pillars carried in front of Egyptian temples.

(ii) The doctrine of the Mind or Nous has also been traced to the "Open Eye" used in Egyptian temples and modern Masonic lodges to symbolize the omniscience and omnipotence of the Egyptian God Osiris.

(iii) The doctrine of the Demiurge and created Gods have also been traced to Atom the Sun God in the creation story of the Memphite Theology of the Egyptians.

(iv) The doctrine of the Summum Bonum or Greatest Good has been shown to be identical with the theory of salvation of the Egyptian Mystery System. The salvation of the soul was the purpose of philosophy, whose methods of purification lifted the individual from the level of a mortal and advanced him to the level of a God. This goal was the Summum Bonum or Greatest Good.

(v) The doctrine of the Ideal State whose attributes have been compared with the attributes of the soul and justice which are contained in the allegory of the charioteer and winged steeds, points to Egyptian origin because the allegory has been traced to the Judgment Drama of the Egyptian Book of the Dead.

(vi) The doctrines of virtue and wisdom have been shown to have originated from the Egyptian Mystery System which required ten virtues in order to subjugate the ten bodily impediments.

7. *Aristotle*

1. *The life of Aristotle is one of discrepancies and doubts.*

(i) While like other philosophers, history does not know any thing about his early life and education, yet it tells the strange story that he spent 20 years as a pupil under Plato, that he never went to Egypt and that Alexander the Great gave him the money to secure the vast number of books which are attached to his name. But history also tells us that Plato was a philosopher and that Aristotle was a scientist and consequently we are forced to ask the question: why should a man like Aristotle waste 20 years of his life under a Teacher who was incompetent to teach him? These circumstances have led to the suspicion that Aristotle must have spent the greater part of those 20 years in advancing his education in Egypt and in accompanying Alexander the Great on his invasion of Egypt, when he got the opportunity to ransack the library at Alexandria and carry off all the books which he wanted. The story of history does not make much sense; but unfortunately throws a cloud of darkness over the life of Aristotle.

(ii) Another discrepancy is to be found in connection with three lists of books said to belong to him, but which differ in source, in date and in quantity, (a) His own list which must receive the date in which he lived: the 4th century B. C. This contains the smallest number of books. (b) A list from Hermippus of Alexandria two centuries later, i. e., 200 B. C. containing 400 books and (c) A list from Arabian sources, compiled at Alexandria, three centuries later, i. e., 1st century A. D. containing a thousand books. One is forced to ask the questions: Did Aristotle write a thousand books in his life time? How has his small list increased after his death to 400 after the lapse of two centuries, and to one thousand after the lapse of five centuries? These circumstances make the authorship of Aristotle very doubtful, for it is incredible that a single individual could write a thousand books on the various fields of science in a single life time.

2. *The doctrines of Aristotle have all been shown to originate from the Egyptian Mystery System*

(i) The doctrine of Being in the metaphysical realm has been explained as the relation between potentiality and actuality, which acts according to the principle of opposites. The Egyptians were the first scientists to discover the principle of duality in nature and therefore represented it by male and female Gods and by pairs of pillars in front of their temples. This is the source of this doctrine.

(ii) In the proof of the existence of God, Aristotle used two doctrines, (a) Teleology, showing purpose and design in nature as the work of an Intelligence and (b) the Unmoved Mover. Both doctrines have been traced to the creation story of the Memphite Theology of the Egyptians where it is shown that creation moved from chaos to order and indicated the work of an Intelligence; and also where Atom the Demiurge and Logos while sitting unmoved upon the

Primeval Hill projected eight Gods from various parts of His body and thus became the Unmoved Mover.

(iii) The doctrine of the origin of the world, according to Aristotle, states that the world is eternal because matter, motion and time are eternal. This same view was expressed by Democritus in 400 B. C. in the dictum ex nihillo nihil fit (out of nothing, nothing comes), indicating that matter is permanent and eternal. The same view has been traced to the creation story of the Memphite Theology of the Egyptians in which chaos or primitive matter is represented by the Primeval Ocean Nun out of which arose the Primeval Hill. These are supposed to have always been in existence.

(iv) The doctrines of the attributes of nature, according to Aristotle, states that nature consists of motion and rest and that the motion moves from the less perfect to the more perfect by a definite law. I suppose the law of evolution. This teaching however did not originate from Aristotle for the problem of motion and rest permanence and change were not only investigated by the Eleatic and later Ionic philosophers, but by the Egyptians in whose creation story, the Memphite Theology, nature is shown to move from chaos by gradual steps to order. Certainly the doctrine of the attributes of nature came from the Egyptians.

(v) The doctrine of the soul, according to Aristotle, states that the soul is a radical principle of life which is identical with the body, and possesses five attributes, being sensitive, rational, nutritive, appetitive and locomotive. Other philosophers have defined the soul (a) as material and composed of fire atoms (b) as a harmony of the body through the blending of opposites, and (c) as the breath of life in the creation story of Genesis. The true source of Aristotle's doctrine of the soul has however been traced to the philosophy of the soul found in the Egyptian Book of the Dead. There we find the soul explained as a unity of nine inseparable souls in one just like the Ennead a God Head of Nine in One, with necessary bodies. In this Egyptian philosophy, the attributes of the soul of the physical body have been found to coincide with those described by Aristotle, and it therefore shows the Egyptian source of Aristotle's doctrine, which relates to a small fragment of the Egyptian philosophy of the soul.

ARGUMENT VI. *The Education of the Egyptian Priests and the Curriculum of the Mystery System show that Egypt was the source of Higher Education in the ancient world, not Greece.*

The first idea that we get from chapter seven is the fact that the Institution of Holy Orders originated from the Egyptian Mystery

[173]

System, where African Priests were organized into various Orders and trained according to their rank. This made the priesthood the custodians of learning until the dawn of the modern age and pointed to Africans as the first professors in Higher Education. The second idea that we get is that the Seven Liberal Arts also originated from the Egyptian Mystery System, because these subjects formed the basis of the education of the Priests, who in addition, had to be versed in the 42 Books of Hermes and to specialize in Magic, Hieroglyphics, secret language and mathematical symbolism. The third idea that we get is that the Curriculum of the Egyptian Mystery System was coextensive with the needs of the highest civilization of the ancient world. Its text books consisted of:—

(i) The 42 Books of Hermes.

(ii) The therapeutic use of the Seven Liberal Arts, for the cure of man's soul.

(iii) The applied Sciences and Arts as revealed by the monuments such as sculpture, painting, drawing, architecture, engineering.

(iv) The social Sciences appropriate for trade and commerce, such as geography, economics and ship-building.

ARGUMENT VII. *The Memphite Theology contains the theology, philosophy and cosmology of the Egyptians and is therefore an authoritative source of doctrinal origin.*

Chapter VIII attempts to show that the Memphite Theology of the Egyptians is the source of (i) Greek philosophy by showing that the separate doctrines of philosophers are portions of the teachings contained in it and also the source of (ii) modern scientific hypotheses by showing that (a) the Nebular Hypothesis and (b) the assumption that there are nine major planets of the solar system have originated from Atom the Egyptian Sun God or Fire God who has been shown to be identical with the atom of modern science. It is because of this great revelation, i. e., the identity of Atom the Sun God of the Egyptians with the atom of modern science that I have recommended the Memphite Theology as a new field of scientific research, and magic the scientific method of the Mysteries as the key to its interpretation. My second reason is the fact that the Memphite Theology is the first Heliocentric theory of the universe, and my third reason is the fact that the history of philosophy is the history of science.

IX. *The New Philosophy of African Redemption*

Chapter IX deals with the New Philosophy of African Redemption, the aim of which is mental and social redemption, by converting the world to the New Philosophy that the Black people of North Africa gave philosophy to the world, but not the Greeks; and by refusing not only to worship Greek intellect, because it is a process of mis-education, but also refusing to submit any longer to missionary policy. The New Philosophy of African Redemption is a necessary escape of the Black people from their social plight caused by a false tradition concerning them which has been set in motion by (a) Alexander the Great (b) Aristotle and his school and (c) Emperors Theodosius and Justinian whose edicts abolished the Egyptian Mysteries: the Greatest Educational and Ecclesiastical System that the world has ever known and established Christianity as its perpetual rival.

NOTES

CHAPTER I

(1) *The Teachings of the Egyptians.* This was called Sophia by the Greeks and meant Wisdom Teaching. It included (a) Philosophy and the Arts and Sciences (b) religion and magic and (c) secret methods of communication both linguistic and mathematical. Read The Stromata of Clement of Alexandria, Bk. 6, p. 756 and 758; also Diodorus I, 80; also Ancient Mysteries by C. H. Vail, p. 22-23; The Stromata of Clement of Alexandria, Bk. 5, c. 7 and 9.

(2) *The Peri Physeos*
This was the name given to one of the earliest books on science apart from the manuscripts of the Egyptians. The name means "Concerning nature". Read Ancient Mysteries by C. H. Vail, p. 16.

CHAPTER II

The period of Greek philosophy was unsuitable for the production of Greek philosophers. Because (a) Persian domination did not only enslave the Greeks but kept them in a constant state of fear (b) It also kept them busy organizing Leagues in constant self-defense against aggression and (c) The city states could not agree, and the Peloponnesian wars kept them in constant warfare with each other. Read Sandford's Mediterranean World, c. 12, p. 203, 205; c. 13 and 15, p. 225, 255; also c. 18, p. 317, 319; also The Tutorial History of Greece, c. 27, 28 and 29.

CHAPTER III

(1) *The Summum Bonum.* This means (a) The Greatest Good (b) the lifting of man from the level of a mortal and advancing him to the level of a God (c) the salvation of the soul (d) the purpose of philosophy (e) the goal of the Egyptian theory of salvation. Read C. H. Vail's Ancient Mysteries, p. 25.

(2) *The Grand Lodge of Luxor*
The ruins of the ancient Grand Lodge of Luxor are found today on the banks of the Nile in Upper Egypt in the ancient city of Thebes. It was built by Pharaoh Amenothis III. It was the only Grand Lodge of the ancient world. It had branches or minor lodges throughout the ancient world; in Europe, Asia, Afrcia, North America, South America

[176]

and probably in Australia. These were some of the places:— (a) Palestine at Mt. Carmel (b) Syria at Mt. Herman in Lebanon (c) Babylon (d) Media, near the Red Sea (e) India, on the banks of the Ganges (f) Burma (g) Athens (h) Rome (i) Croton (j) Rhodes (k) Delphi (l) Miletus (m) Cyprus (n) Corinth (o) Crete (p) Central and South America, especially Peru (q) Among the American Indians and among the Mayas, Aztecs and Incas of Mexico. Read Encyclopaedia of Religion and Ethics by Jas. Hastings; Lives of Eminent Philosophers by Diogenes Laertius; and History of Philosophy by Thomas Stanley. The discovery of the ruins of Luxor on the banks of the Nile and the organization of the Egyptian Mysteries into a Grand Lodge with minor lodges throughout the ancient world are evidence that Egypt was the cradle of the Mysteries and of the Masonic Brotherhood.

(3) *The rebuilding of the temple of Delphi*
This temple was burnt down in 548 B. C. by the Greeks who were always hostile towards the Egyptian Mysteries. The Brethren tried at first to raise funds from the native Greeks but failed in their attempt. They then decided to approach the Grand Master Amasis King of Egypt, who unhesitatingly donated three times as much as was needed for the purpose. This act of King Amasis shows the universality of the brotherhood of the Egyptian Mysteries and of Free Masonry. Read Sandford's Mediterranean World, p. 135 and 139; also John Kendrick's Ancient Egypt, Bk. II, p. 363.

(4) *The abolition of Greek philosophy together with the Egyptian Mysteries*
Identical effects proceed from identical causes. Therefore the edicts of Theodosius in the 4th century A. D. and of Justinian in the 6th century A. D., which closed down the Egyptian Mysteries, simultaneously had the same effect upon Greek philosophy, and proved the identity between them. Read The Ecclesiastical edicts of the Theodosian Code by W. K. Boyd; also Mythology of Egypt by Max Muller, c. 13, p. 241-245; also Sandford's Mediterranean World, p. 508, 548, 552-568.

(5) *The Statue of the Egyptian Goddess Isis with Her Child Horus in Her arms*
This was the first Madonna and Child of human history. It was a Black Madonna and Child. Read Max Muller's Mythology of Egypt, c. 13, p. 241-245; also Sandford's Mediterranean World, p. 552-568. Remember that the name Egyptian is a Greek word Aiguptos which means Black, and that primitive man visualized God in terms of his own attributes and this included colour.

[177]

(6) *All the great religious leaders from Moses to Christ were Initiates of the Egyptian Mysteries*

This is an inference from the nature of the Egyptian Mysteries and prevailing custom.

(a) The Egyptian Mystery System was the One Holy Catholic Religion of the remotest antiquity.

(b) It was the one and only Masonic Order of Antiquity, and as such,

(c) It built the Grand Lodge of Luxor in Egypt and encompassed the ancient world with its branch lodges.

(d) It was the first University of history and it made knowledge a secret, so that all who desired to become Priests and Teachers had to obtain their training from the Mystery System, either locally at a branch lodge or by travelling to Egypt.

We know that Moses became an Egyptian Priest, a Hierogrammat, and that Christ after attending the lodge at Mt. Carmel went to Egypt for Final Initiation, which took place in the Great Pyramid of Cheops. Other religious leaders obtained their preparation from lodges most convenient to them.

(e) This explains why all religions, seemingly different, have a common nucleus of similarity; belief in a God; belief in immortality and a code of ethics. Read Ancient Mysteries by C. H. Vail, p. 61; Mystical Life of Jesus by H. Spencer Lewis; Esoteric Christianity by Annie Besant, p. 107, 128-129; Philo; also read note (2) Chapter III for branch lodges of the ancient world.

CHAPTER IV

(1) *The Genesis of Greek Enlightenment*

In the reign of King Amasis, the Persians through Cambyses invaded Egypt 525 B. C. and as a result (a) Immigration regulations against the Greeks were removed (b) They were allowed to settle at Naucratis and do their research (c) This contact enabled the Greeks to begin to borrow Egyptian Culture and to become enlightened. Read Herodotus, Bk. II, p. 113; Plutarch, p. 380; Diogenes, Bk. IX 49; Ovid Fasti III 338.

(2) *Cheops and Cecrops*

Those were Greek names for the Egyptian Khufu who belonged to the 4th Dynasty of the Egyptians. It was during the Pyramid Age, and Cheops was also the name of the Great Pyramid where Christ received His Final Initiation into the Egyptian Mysteries. Read Brucker's Critical History of Philosophy; also Mystical Life of Jesus by H. Spencer Lewis.

STOLEN LEGACY

CHAPTER V

(1) *The Diagram of the Four Qualities and Four Elements*
This is important evidence that the teachings of the supposed early
Ionic philosophers and of Heracleitus originated from the Egyptian
Mysteries. Read the Diagram and also Ancient Mysteries by C. H.
Vail, p. 61; and the Creation Story of the Memphite Theology by
Frankfort; also Rosicrucian Digest, May 1952, p. 175.

(2) *The Pythagorean Theorem*
Pythagoras travelled to Egypt and was taught geometry by the
Egyptian Priests and made to sacrifice to the Gods, before they showed
him the proof of the theorem of the square on the hypotenuse of a
right angled triangle. Pythagoras did not discover this proof, and it is
misleading to name the theorem after him. Read Herodotus, Bk. III,
p. 124; Diogenes, Bk. VIII, p. 3; Pliny, N. H., 36, 9; also Plutarch
and Demetrius.

CHAPTER VI

(1) *The doctrine of self-knowledge: Man know thyself (Seauton
gnothi)*
This doctrine has been falsely ascribed to Socrates. It was an inscription that was placed on the Egyptian temples, and Socrates copied
it directly or indirectly. Read Zeller's History of Philosophy, p. 105;
S. Clymer's Fire Philosophy and Max Muller's Egyptian Mythology.

(2) *The Farewell Conversation of Socrates with his pupils and
friends*
These conversations are significant in the following respects:—

(a) Socrates is identified as a member of the Egyptian Mysteries or
Masonic Order.

(b) Masonic behavior is manifested through these conversations.

(c) The books containing these conversations; Plato's Crito, Phaedo,
Euthyphro, Apology and Timaeus, are the earliest specimen of Masonic
literature apart from the secret writings of the Egyptians.

(d) Of the three Athenian philosophers Socrates stood highest in
the rank of a Free Mason. He was not afraid of death, he did not
publish the knowledge imparted to him and he was an honest man.
Read Crito and Phaedo of Plato.

(3) *Plato's Theory of Ideas*
After the Egyptian Priests discovered the fundamental principle of
opposites as underlying life in the universe, they applied it in their
interpretation of natural phenomena. Consequently this mode of interpretation has been reflected in the teachings of the so-called Greek
philosophers who had obtained their education from the Egyptian

[179]

Mystery System. Read the doctrines of Parmenides who in the problem of existence distinguishes between Being and non-Being; also of Heracleitus in the problem of flux and change through the process of transmutation; also of Socrates in the proof of immortality, and Plato in his supposed Theory of Ideas, in which he distinguished between (a) the real and unreal (b) the idea of a thing and the thing itself (c) the noumena and phenomena. In all these instances the principle of opposites has been used as a method of interpretation. This method is Egyptian not Platonic.

(4) *The Republic of Plato*: *The Ideal State*

Plato's authorship of the Republic is disputed for the following reasons:—

(a) The attributes of an Ideal State are expressed in the allegory of the charioteer and winged steeds which is dramatized in the Judgment Drama of the Egyptian Book of the Dead and therefore proves its Egyptian origin.

(b) The chariot was neither a culture pattern nor war machine of the Greeks at the time of Plato. The wars of the Greeks with the Persians and the Peloponnesian wars were all maritime.

(c) At this time the Egyptians were specialists in the manufacture of chariots and horse breeding Gen., c. 45, v. 27; c. 47, v. 17; Deut., c. 17, v. 16; I Kings, c. 10, v. 28.

(d) The historians Diogenes Laertius, Aristoxenus and Favorinus have declared that the subject matter of the Republic was found in the controversies written by Protagoris (481-411) when Plato was but a boy. Read Diogenes Laertius, p. 311 and 327; also The Egyptian Book of the Dead, c. 17; also Republic III 415; V 478; and VI 490 sqq.

(5) *The Timaeus of Plato*

Plato's authorship of the Timaeus is also disputed for the following reasons:—

(a) The historian Diogenes Laertius in Bk. VIII, p. 399-401 has declared that when Plato visited Dionysius in Sicily, he paid Philolaus a Pythagorean forty Alexandrian Minae of silver for a book, from which he copied the whole contents of the Timaeus.

(b) The subject matter of the Timaeus is eclectic. Read the Timaeus.

(6) *Magic is the Key to the interpretation of ancient religion and natural philosophy*

Through the application of the principle: that the qualities of entities, human or divine, are distributed throughout their various parts; and that contact with such entities releases those qualities, many religious phenomena and those of primitive science could be interpreted and understood.

[180]

(a) The cure of the woman who touched the hem of Christ's garment, Mark, c. 5, verses 25-34.

(b) The cure of several people, who held the handkerchiefs of St. Paul. Acts, c. 19, verse 12.

(c) In order to accomplish creation, Atom the Sun God sat upon Ptah, the God of Gods, in order to absorb His qualities of creative thought, speech and omnipotence. This act qualified Him as the Logos and Demiurge and He first created the Gods and finally mortals. Read Memphite Theology in Frankfort's Ancient Egyptian Religion and Dr. Frazer's Golden Bough.

(7) *The doubts and discrepancies in the life and activities of Aristotle*

It is somewhat unfortunate that history has represented the life and activities of Aristotle in a way so repugnant to reason, that the world has been compelled to doubt his accomplishments and fame. It tells us that

(a) he spent twenty years as a pupil under Plato whom we know was incompetent to teach him.

(b) It tells us that Alexander gave him money to buy his large number of books, but the Greeks had no libraries at the time, nor was it easy to purchase books which were not in circulation.

(c) It also tells us that three lists of books which bear his name differ from one another, in source, date and quantity.

(d) The third list contains one thousand books: a quantity which is a mental and physical impossibility as the production of a single individual in a single lifetime.

(e) It is silent about Aristotle's visits to Egypt, although it was the custom in his days for Greek students to go to Egypt for the purpose of their education. Read Zeller's History of Philosophy, p. 172-173; Diogenes, Bk. V, p. 449; B. D. Alexander's History of Philosophy, p. 92-93.

(8) *The Unmoved Mover: Proton Kinoun Akineton*

A doctrine ascribed to Aristotle in his attempt to prove the existence of God. The God in this doctrine was Atom the Egyptian Sun God, who in the creation story of the Memphite Theology, sat upon the God of Gods Ptah and having absorbed His creative qualities, speech and omnipotence, became the Logos and accomplished the work of creation by projecting Gods from various parts of His own body. This doctrine did not originate from Aristotle, but has been traced to the creation story of the Memphite Theology of the Egyptians. Read Memphite Theology in Frankfort's Ancient Egyptian Religion, c. 20 and

23; also p. 25, 26 and 35; William Turner's History of Philosophy, p. 141-143; B. D. Alexander, p. 102-103.

(9) *Aristotle's doctrine of the Soul*

This doctrine has been found to be only a very small part of the elaborate philosophy of the soul found in the Egyptian Book of the Dead, which is the original source of Aristotle's supposed doctrine. Read the Egyptian Book of the Dead by Sir E. A. Budge, p. 29-64.

CHAPTER VII

The Curriculum of the Egyptian Mysteries

Through the curriculum of the Egyptian Mysteries it is now known that the African Continent has given the following Legacy to the civilization of the world. It consists of the following culture patterns:—

(1) Holy Catholic Orders, together with a priesthood divided into ranks according to training.

(2) Holy Catholic Worship, consisting of rituals, ceremonies including processions and appropriate vestments of priests.

(3) Greek Philosophy and the Arts and Sciences, including the Seven Liberal Arts, that is, the Quadrivium and Trivium which were the foundation training of Neophytes. These were included in the forty-two Books of Hermes.

(4) The applied Sciences which produced the pyramids, tombs, libraries, obelisks, and Sphinxes, war chariots and ships, etc.

(5) The social sciences, appropriate for the highest civilization in ancient times. Read The Stromata of Clement of Alexandria, c. 6, p. 756, 758; also Diodorus I, 80. Read also The Mechanical Triumphs of the Ancient Egyptians by F. M. Barber; History of Mathematics by Florian Cajeri; History of Mathematics by W. W. R. Ball.

CHAPTER VIII

The Memphite Theology

(1) *Definition*

The Memphite Theology is an inscription on a stone containing the cosmology, theology and philosophy of the Egyptians. Read Frankfort's Ancient Egyptian Religion, c. 20 and 23; also Frankfort's Intellectual Adventure of Man. It is located in the British Museum.

(2) *Importance*

Its importance lies in the fact that (a) it is an authoritative source of Egyptian Philosophy, Cosmology and Religion (b) it is proof of the Egyptian origin of Greek philosophy.

(3) *The Source of Modern Scientific Knowledge*

(a) Atom the Egyptian Sun God who is the Logos of Heracleitus, the Demiurge of Plato and the Unmoved Mover of Aristotle creates eight other Gods by projecting them from His own body, thus producing nine Gods or the Ennead. This is identical with the Nebular Hypothesis of Laplace, in which the original Sun creates eight other planets, by throwing off rings from itself, thus producing the nine major planets of modern scientific belief.

(b) It has been shown on pages 146 and 147 of this book, that the name of Atom the Egyptian Sun God is the same name used for the atom of science and also that the attributes of both are the same. Read Frankfort's Intellectual Adventure of Man, p. 53; Frankfort's Kingship and the Gods, p. 182; also Herodotus II, 112; Diodorus I, 29.

(4) *It offers great possibilities for modern scientific research*

What science knows about (a) the number of major planets (b) how these major planets were created by the Sun and (c) the attributes of the atom has been traced to the Cosmology of the Memphite Theology, which suggests that (d) science knows only 1/5 of the secrets of creation and therefore 4/5 of such secrets yet remains to be discovered (e) consequently The Memphite Theology offers great possibilities for modern scientific research.

CHAPTER IX

The Drama of Greek Philosophy

(1) This consists of three actors (a) Alexander the Great who invaded Egypt and plundered the Royal Library at Alexandria (b) Aristotle and the alumni of his school, who took possession of the Royal Library and having first carried off large quantities of scientific books, subsequently converted it into a research Centre and University. (c) The Roman government, which through the edicts of Emperors Theodosius and Justinian closed down the Egyptian Mysteries together with its schools, the University of the Ancient World and System of the African Culture.

(2) The result of this was (a) the misrepresentation and erroneous opinion that the African Continent and people are backward in culture and have made no contribution to civilization and (b) the establishment of Christianity as a rival against the Mysteries or African System of Culture, in order to perpetuate this erroneous opinion.

(3) A further result has been (a) the false worship of Greek intellect and (b) the activities of Missionary enterprise through which the culture of Black people is caricatured both in literature and in exhibitions.

(4) A further result has been (a) the general feeling among Black

people throughout the world that they are in great need of freedom from their social plight, and (b) The offer by "Stolen Legacy" of a "New Philosophy of African Redemption" in order to meet this universal need of "Social Reformation".

(5) *The nature and methods of this New Philosophy and Social Reformation*

(a) The New Philosophy of African Redemption is simply the proposition that the "Greeks were not the authors of Greek philosophy: but the people of North Africa, the Egyptians". This must be preached and circulated for centuries to come.

(b) The effects of this New Philosophy should be as follows:—

(1) To change the mentality both of White and Black people and their attitude towards each other and bring about a Social Reformation.

(2) To stimulate the Black people to abandon their false worship of Greek intellect, and to reject the caricature of their culture by Missionary enterprise and to demand a change in Missionary policy.

INDEX

STOLEN LEGACY